NIGEL HARRIS is Professor Emeritus of the Economics of the City, University College, London and author of *The End of the Third World*, *The New Untouchables* and *The Return of Cosmopolitan Capital* (all I.B.Tauris).

Thinking the Unthinkable

The Immigration Myth Exposed

Nigel Harris

I.B.Tauris *Publishers*
LONDON • NEW YORK

Published in 2002 by I.B.Tauris & Co Ltd
6 Salem Road, London W2 4BU
175 Fifth Avenue, New York NY 10010
www.ibtauris.com

In the United States and Canada distributed by St. Martin's Press
175 Fifth Avenue, New York NY 10010

ISBN 1 86064 672 7 hardback
      1 86064 671 9 paperback

A full CIP record for this book is available from the British Library
A full CIP record for this book is available from the Library of Congress

Library of Congress catalog card: available

Typeset in Palatino by Dexter Haven Associates, London
Printed and bound in Great Britain by MPG Books Ltd, Bodmin, Cornwall

Contents

Preface

In developed countries, the policy debate on immigration controls is for the first time in a long time beginning to open up. The reasons for this are discussed later in this book. But the debate at the moment assumes the value of controls and concentrates on what kind of controls are the best. It assumes that governments can foresee how many workers will be needed in the future, and of what types, and can employ migration controls to select those it needs while protecting the needs of its citizens. This is at the moment 'common-sense', even though experience suggests the reverse. This book seeks to set out the evidence as to why this is so, why governments should – and will be obliged to – begin to move towards the ending of controls altogether, moving back to the situation before the twentieth century when in general the world enjoyed freedom to move and work as people wished.

The perspective is in aspiration global. Or rather it seeks to deal with immigration to the developed countries as a common issue, eliciting similar responses and arguments; that is, the control of migration is systematic rather than peculiar to one country or another. But it is written in one place, London, so inevitably local experience looms large – and no doubt distorts the reading of what is common. The framework for Britain assumes Europe. On the other hand, the quality of research and argument on international migration is more advanced and sophisticated in the US than in much of Europe, so the use of American experience is important in the arguments. Japan and Australia appear at various points as illustration of particular themes, but without adequate treatment in their own right. Finally, a concern with migration to the developed countries of Europe, North America, Japan and the rest cannot be separated from emigration from developing countries – how does one relate to the other, and to the overriding global objective of the reduction in world poverty?

The issues are both simple and very complicated. This book is directed at as broad an audience as possible. To ease access, most references have been omitted. This is most unjust to the authors and sources on which the argument depends. Some suggested reading and references at the end go a little way to acknowledge the debts without which this work could not have been written, but it is only a nominal marker.

Many people have contributed, most in discussions over many years, particularly around my earlier foray into the field (*The New Untouchables*, 1995). For this work, I owe especial thanks to Simone Lucatello for his direct contributions, and to Kate Harris for careful scrutiny. Zoe Harper of Asylum Aid and Jean Kandler of the press office of the Refugee Council were also particularly helpful. The enthusiasm and timely stories of Turi Munthe at I.B.Tauris sustained flagging spirits on the way. Nigel Fountain provided a crucial story. To these and all others, many thanks – of course, errors of fact and judgement must exclusively be claimed my own.

Nigel Harris

Glossary of Acronyms

AFL–CIO   American Federation of Labour–Congress of Industrial Organisations, the leading trade union federation in the US

GATT   General Agreement on Trade and Tariffs, main authority for the regulation of world trade, until superseded by the World Trade Organisation

ILO   International Labour Office, main UN agency concerned with the conditions of work and workers

INS   Immigration and Naturalisation Service, agency of the US Government for the control and regulation of immigration etc

IOM   International Organisation for Migration, UN agency responsible for research and policy advice on international migration

IT   information technology

MITI   Ministry of International Trade and Industry (Government of Japan)

NAFTA   North American Free Trade Agreement, the agreement between Canada, the US and Mexico on free trade between the three

NGO   non-government organisation

OECD   Main organisation of the governments of the developed countries for the regulation of economic relations, research and recommendations on economic policy to its members. It includes some of the leading developing countries: Turkey, South Korea, Mexico

TUC   Trades Union Congress, Britain's trade union federation

UNHCR   UN High Commission for Refugees, the main world organisation for the management and care of refugees; primarily focussed on those who leave their countries rather than the internally displaced

WTO   World Trade Organisation, the main authority for the regulation of world trade (superseding GATT, see above)

List of Tables and Figures

Tables

Figures

Prologue

The wrong kind of deaths: part I

Three days after Christmas Day 1996, 182 dazed, shabby and hungry Asians wandered into the village of Ermioni in Greece. They had been offloaded from a ship at gunpoint the previous night.

They had a story to tell the Greek police. They had set out at different times. The Pakistanis, paying US$4,000, set out on 26 September and flew to Antakya in Turkey. The Sri Lankans, paying US$8,000, left Colombo for Cairo, then drove to Alexandria, where they paid a further US$1,000 to the harbour agent. The Indians, paying US$5,000, flew to Larnaca in Cyprus. A ship, the *Yiohan*, picked them up one by one on Christmas Eve, loading up with around 88 Pakistanis, 149 Sri Lankans and 227 Indians.

The 1,500-tonne *Yiohan*, registered in Honduras, had once been a trawler, and the 460-odd passengers were packed in the former fish tanks, fed on a crust of bread and half a cup of water per day. The captain was Youssef al-Halal, a 38-year-old Lebanese married to a Greek woman, and the crew comprised three other Greeks.

A small boat, the F174, with a two-member crew, set out from Malta to meet the *Yiohan* halfway between Malta and Sicily to ferry the migrants to Sicily. At three o'clock in the morning of Christmas Day, the first Indians were offloaded on to the F174. The boat's capacity was about 100, but loading continued at gunpoint until around 320 were packed on and many fell to their deaths. The captain was very drunk.

'People were desperately screaming for help,' said survivor Ahmad Shahab. His tears flowed freely as he continued: 'I saw my brother go down. I yelled, 'Please, please, he can't swim!' But people just looked. Oh, how will I tell my father? How will I tell my father?

The two crew then abandoned the F174 and climbed aboard the *Yiohan*. It is not clear whether the captain had always intended to ram the F174 or if it was an accident. But following a collision the boat sank swiftly, with the migrants trapped in the cabin. Twenty-nine managed to leap off and grab ropes on the *Yiohan*, but some 283 were killed. The *Yiohan* continued to Greece and dumped what was left of her cargo at the first point possible. She then disappeared.

The story was so incredible, nobody believed it for two weeks. Who would believe the survivors? They were:

> Just a bunch of illegal immigrants, on the run, wading from beaches or hiding in trees. They had no power. They were the kind of people who got caught, or killed, all the time, being landed on the wrong islands or in the wrong country or wandering on to mined beaches, or being dumped overboard. No one cared.

> Euan Ferguson, *Observer*, 12 January 1997

> Many died, but they were the wrong kind of dead. Fortress Europe does not want to know what's happening on its shores; it doesn't want to accept people are dying, daily, because of co-ordinated draconian immigration laws, many drawn up in a spirit of populism rather than humanity. The dead were acting illegally and they were black. And no one cared.

> Euan Ferguson, *Observer*, 19 January 1997

The wrong kind of deaths: part II

The village of Tordher, with a population of 30,000, situated between the Kabul and Indus rivers in the Northwest Frontier Province of Pakistan, first heard the news via a crackling telephone call from Greece. Shakoor Ahmed, his voice choking with sobs, told them that Abid, Zahir, Rais, Fahim, Fazal, Iqtidar, Moin, Habib and other boys, all from Tordher, were dead.

> Every home in Tordher has been affected...

> On the day after Shakoor's phone call, the chaos of pony-traps, bicycles, tractors and 3-wheel pick-ups that normally chokes the main bazaar

came to a stop. Shops and stalls closed for two days, and the schools and offices were shuttered.

'It was a kind of doomsday,' Mr Aslam, Municipal Committee chief, said. 'Those kids were very popular. People gathered on corners, remembering their good acts.'

By Pakistan standards, Tordher is not poor. It stands on rich, alluvial soil...

It educates most of its children to high school level: most of the victims had matriculated and several had degrees...

Habib, 27, who was married with four children, returned from work in Italy to Tordher in 1995. The pressure on him to go back was intense. His father, Zabi Ullah, is a candidate in next month's general election...another son is studying medicine in Moscow, requiring thousands of pounds a year, while his two unmarried daughters will need dowries. Life in Italy is hard. Habib's four cousins earn about £700 a month on building sites, far below the going rate for Italian labour. Of this, they spend just £250 on themselves; the rest goes back to Pakistan where each supports nine or 10 relatives. In Tordher, however...families with relatives abroad are rich...

Lost with Habib were two of his closest friends, Fazal Maula and Iqtidar Ali. The three were famous locally as stars of the village cricket team. 'Life in Tordher revolves around the mosque and the cricket team,' Mr Aslam said.

Many of the bereaved families who scrimped and mortgaged themselves to the hilt to pay the agent now face penury...

Entirely dehumanised, the migrants remain mere statistics even when they die. Who were these 'bogus migrants'? Not just cricketers, but men such as Abid Hussein, a social sciences honours graduate and a trained paramedic who, like his two brothers, despaired of finding a job, and Iqtidar Ali, four years unemployed after taking honours in his B.Sc. – his graduate brother who speaks fluent English is the only one working in the family, reading electricity meters for £60 a month.

David Rose, *Observer*, 2 January 1997

A tiny chill of reality

On 18 June 2000, a customs officer at Eastern Docks, Dover, opened the back of a white Mercedes articulated container truck carrying tomatoes from Zeebrugge in Belgium. He found inside 58 corpses, 54 men and four women, with two survivors, all Chinese.

On the hottest day of the year, novice driver Perry Wacker, 32, of Rotterdam, failed to switch on the cooling system. A survivor recalled the desperate screaming and clawing at the sides as the majority died – leaving enough air for just two to survive.

They had journeyed for four months from Fujian province, via Moscow and across the Czech mountains. The destination of the group was restaurants in Newport Street in London's Chinatown. There they hoped to get £167 per week and pay off in two years or so the debts incurred for the journey. There is a great shortage of workers there since many second generation Chinese go to universities and work in the professions.

The British government held the smugglers responsible, and accused the Belgian authorities of incompetence for releasing a group of Chinese detained there in April. The Chinese government said Western countries encouraged the racketeers by granting political asylum. 'Certain countries,' warned a Chinese foreign ministry spokesman, 'should learn from this tragedy'.

> Like many villages in the south-eastern provinces of China, Fuqing has seen changes in the past few years. Now there are concrete pavements and a newly landscaped town square. A care and cultural centre for senior citizens has recently been opened. Above the traditional squat brick houses rise six-storey mansions topped by huge white satellite dishes and full of crystal and gold.
>
> On a burnished plaque on the wall of a clothes shop an inscription praises a local hero: a 22-year-old who two years ago left his home to seek his fortune in Europe. He was the man who funded the street improvements. A cornerstone in the old people's centre lauds the generosity of another expatriate.
>
> The number of people who have left Fuqing and Changle – the nearby town that was home to most of the 54 men and four women found dead...has led to the coining of a morbid nickname. Fuqing and Changle are, the locals say, 'widows' villages'.
>
> On 19 February, a smartly dressed 19-year-old called Chen Lin left his Fuqing home and walked to the railway station. He took a train to

Beijing…He was, close relatives say, entirely in the hands of the sh'e tau' – or 'snakeheads' – the local gang leaders who run the human trafficking trade. His family had paid them the equivalent of £14,000 to get Chen Lin to the UK. With his death, it will take them five years to pay off the debt…

Do we blame the parents who, hoping for a better life for their children, save for years to send their best and brightest to the West? Or the traffickers who, often having made the journey themselves, decide to look for faster ways to get rich than washing dishes in a restaurant? Or the Western governments who have failed to tackle the problem?

Observer, 25 June 2000

Fragments I: getting into Fortress Europe

The corpses of several hundred trafficked women – strangled, shot or beaten to a pulp – fetch up around Europe each year. Many more bodies, Europol reckons, are never found. The organised gangs of traffickers who lure and smuggle young women, mostly from Eastern and Central Europe, into prostitution are ruthless. In January, a group of 22 women being led across a mountain range into Greece via Bulgaria were abandoned by their traffickers when a blizzard struck. Two women froze to death before Greek border troops could reach them.

Economist, October 1999

A young woman's body was found attached to a deflated dinghy abandoned in the Adriatic in mid-January 2000. It confirmed fears that the passengers, 59 illegal immigrants, had drowned on New Year's Eve. The Italian coastguards were accused of ignoring warnings from relatives in Italy that the vessel was missing in rough seas after leaving Albania. No search was launched and the claims were dismissed until the body was sighted about 11 miles from the Albanian island of Sazan. The Albanian authorities interviewed witnesses and confirmed that the boat contained three Albanian smugglers, 13 other Albanians, four Moldovan teenage girls and 39 people of Chinese and Kurdish origin travelling from Iraq and Turkey. The 12-metre boat was supposed to hold 30 people. In an earlier incident, on 27 March 1997, 100 died when an Italian warship, *Zeffiro*, rammed their boat while trying to force it back to Albania.

In April 2000, 13 Afghans and Pakistanis were drowned crossing the river Tisza, separating Hungary from the Ukraine, when their dinghy capsized. In July 1999, 300 Indians, Afghans and Pakistanis were found starving and dehydrated by the Hungarian police on a farm near Budapest. On 15 September 2000, 12 Iranians drowned in the Sava river when their boat capsized as they tried to reach Croatia. Over the preceding two weeks, the Croatian border guards had turned away at least 309 travellers trying to enter from Bosnia.

In July 1995, 18 Sri Lankan Tamils suffocated to death, trapped in a container truck at Gyor, Hungary. In December 1997, 16 Sri Lankan Tamils were discovered dead in a refrigerated container truck on arrival in Britain.

Thirty-two Moroccans and four Algerians were found starving in a truck in southern Spain on their way to farm work. On 11 November 2000, two boats carrying 70 migrants from Morocco, including several children, sank a few yards off the Spanish Canary Island of Fuerteventura. Spanish authorities say that at least 250 have died crossing the Straits of Gibraltar from Morocco to Spain since 1998. In August 2000, the Moroccan daily, *Liberación*, put the number at over 3,000. In May 1997, a Nigerian woman, seven months pregnant, scaled two fences and penetrated a roll of barbed wire to enter the Spanish enclave of Ceuta in Morocco. She was caught, gaoled and committed suicide.

In September 2000, 10 Bangladeshis were found at the Folkestone entrance to the Eurotunnel, having jumped from a UK-bound freight train. Later, a further two men were found in agony with broken legs at the base of a 12-feet fence, having tried to escape. A third was found unconscious with serious head injuries on the railway line close to the tunnel.

Fragments II: getting into Fortress America

Between 1993 and 1997, the border between the US and Mexico became increasingly militarised (Dunn, 1996). There was a 76 per cent increase in the number of border patrol agents, from 3,400 to nearly 6,000, and new equipment, vehicles and helicopters. Thirty-two miles of metal barrier were erected, 33 more miles under construction. As a result, the flow of migrants has been diverted away from established routes to the most dangerous and least populated areas, particularly through the Arizona desert, where there are 30–40 miles to cross, and summer temperatures peak at over 43 degrees centigrade.

One estimate is that 1,600 people died on the US side of the border between 1993 and 1997. In a sample of 1,034 cases: 29 per cent drowned; 15 per cent died on highways; 14 per cent were murdered; 13 per cent died in vehicle accidents; 9 per cent died from environmental conditions such as dehydration; 5 per cent died in train accidents; 4 per cent died from natural causes; and 12 per cent died for unspecified reasons. Men accounted for 85 per cent of those dead, 63 per cent were aged between 20 and 39, and 13 per cent between 10 and 19 (Eschbach, Hagan and Rodriguez, 1999).

When UN Human Rights Commissioner Mary Robinson visited the border in November 1999, she was told deaths occurred almost every day, with 306 recorded so far that year, compared to 23 in 1994. Many were saved by being arrested by the border patrol – 1,041 were rescued from severe difficulties in 1998. The 300 corpses found by the border patrol in 1998 were largely recovered from deserts or at river crossings, but their patrols rarely penetrate the treacherous mountain ranges. A Californian non-governmental organisation constructed a row of two-metre-high crosses for a mile along the border to commemorate the victims.

Efforts by the Immigration and Naturalisation Services (INS) to stem the tide of immigrants was not enough for some. American rancher and cowboy vigilantes formed posses to hunt illegal aliens, mainly in Arizona. The Mexican government reported that 450 had been rounded up by posses of US citizens between January 1999 and May 2000; two were killed and seven injured.

In December 1999, on Interstate Highway 40, a Chevrolet van carrying workers to jobs in Kentucky and Florida crashed, leaving 13 dead and four survivors. Six were from the town of Venustiano Carranza in Mexico. Antonia Lopez, widow of Neftali, was left facing debts of US$2,000, which the family had borrowed to send her husband to the US, as well as a further US$400. Patricia Calvo, with a disabled daughter, also owed US$2,000.

In January 2000, 18 illegal immigrants were discovered in a container arriving in Seattle from Hong Kong. Three of them were dead. It was the third group arrested in recent days. There were 600 Chinese arrivals found in rickety ships en route to the US in 1999. Two separate trailers were intercepted in El Paso, Texas: one held 44 illegal immigrants, the other 21. They had been abandoned after travelling from Central America. Two died of starvation.

In March, three illegal immigrants were found dead, along with 28 survivors, in the freezing mountains of eastern San Diego County. Weekend storms had dropped eight inches of snow and the temperature was below –5 degrees centigrade. In the same month, 18 Chinese men were found in a 40-feet container in the hold of a ship, sitting in darkness on blankets and boxes. They had spent three weeks there. All were dead.

On 13 April, five illegal immigrants died and 48 others hospitalised in southern Mexico. They were en route to the US in search of work, travelling in two sealed cars containing 200 people from Honduras, El Salvador and Guatemala.

On 24 May, 41 illegal immigrants – eight Chinese, five Central Americans and the rest, including a baby, Mexican – were found dead in an abandoned truck trailer in central El Paso, Texas. Border patrol agents found them lying among the freight of second-hand clothes, without food or water.

In June, four days into what she was told would be a six-hour trip, Yolanda González lay dead of dehydration in the Arizona desert, a victim of the 43-degree heat and her determination to save her daughter. The young Mexican mother had given nearly all the water she carried to her 18-month-old. The infant was alive, with only a few drops of water in her bottle, when the border patrol found them. Her mother was the sixth illegal immigrant to die in the Arizona desert that week. Two Mexican youths, pursued by the border patrol, simultaneously drowned in the Rio Grande between the US and Mexico.

Thinking the Unthinkable

Introduction:
The Horrors

The stories are endless, daily accounts of death on the borders. Europeans and Americans need brave hearts to contemplate the slaughter. So numerous are the victims that we no longer think of them as cricketers from Tordher, merry toddlers from Fuqing or shy teenagers from Venustiano Carranza. They rarely have names, only labels: 'illegal immigrants'; 'wetbacks'; 'economic migrants'; 'asylum-seekers'.

Yet some of the stories still have the power to shock, even if only momentarily: 58 killed crossing the English Channel in a container truck; 300 drowned at Christmas in the waters of the Mediterranean; daily casualties along the perimeter of Europe's tormented borders or along the frontier between Mexico and the US.

In the frozen wastes of the high passes of the Pyrenees or the Swiss Alps, across the deserts of Arizona, the Saharan route to Morocco and Spain; across the seas, from Haiti or Cuba to Florida, across the Straits of Gibraltar, the English Channel from France, from Albania to southern Italy; or across the rivers – the Tisza between Hungary and the Ukraine, the Rio Grande snaking across northern Mexico: the crossings are the points where people become 'no-men' in no-man's-land, and subject to great danger. Or to change the image – and the dynamic – where the termites burrow through the walls of the national fortresses – the snakeheads, the coyotes, the brokers shepherding the troops of bedraggled footsore migrants through that no-man's-land while the world sleeps. Their ingenuity in defying the obstacles, in scaling the fortifications, is even more impressive than the fearful structures of intimidation set up to thwart them.

1

The shock is not simply due to the deaths, the maiming of young lives, the grief of parents, widows and orphans. Shocking, too, is the way we have come to accept that this is the way of the world, and the self-righteousness of citizens and governments in the face of such ceaseless brutality. Of course, there are winces as the newspaper is opened, the radio or the television reports broadcast; words of regret, vows that it must never happen again. But even these are commonly lost in the swift attempt by ministers to blame some other government or, those universal objects of hate, the smugglers of people and the traffickers of slaves. Yet these professionals in the craft of clandestinely crossing borders are empowered only by the existence of border controls. Men and women can be destroyed on the barbed wire fences that surround Fortress Europe only because there are barbed wire fences. Attention focuses exclusively, not on the victims hanging on the wire, nor those who put the wire in place, but on the smuggler.

The stories illustrate some of the horrors produced by the system, the cruelty to those seeking work or fleeing terror. But without the papers that guarantee they exist, they lack access to basic human rights. Reported and documented cases may not be the worst and do not depict a comprehensive picture; they are accidental and give no more than a taste of the atrocities. There are very many more that do not catch the eye of a journalist or an official.

It is officially stated that only 2,000 have died on the borders trying to enter Europe in the past decade. Given the daily corpse count, it seems a wild underestimate. Then there are the bodies not found, lost at sea, in the mountains or in the deserts. The US border patrol claims to have discovered 1,600 corpses in the course of four years during the 1990s: the body count of those trying to cross the border. That is far more than the number of Americans killed in the Gulf War. The crash on Interstate 40 at the end of 1999 left another crop of grieving widows, fatherless children, parents without sons, far to the south in a town in central Mexico. Casual statistics make no allowance for the bereaved, or for those who mortgage their family's wealth to send a son or daughter to work in the alien north, who lose a child but retain the crippling debts.

The slaughter of some and the disablement of others is not an act of nature, such as an earthquake, a typhoon or a flood. It is not the result of wars or civil disorder. It is a regime constructed and maintained by the deliberate action of governments, by the calm, sensible and apparently liberal – even kindly – men and women who constitute civil authority. They do not intend the disasters. They probably regret them. Some of them no doubt espouse moral codes that forbid them to kill, that affirm the sanctity of life, that propose compassion for those in need. Yet the laws they have put in place turn all this to hypocrisy.

Why is this system in place? What high ends of public policy could possibly justify this regime of accidental brutality? Could there be matters of interest so vital that, however regrettable, the order must be maintained?

The mystery deepens. Those seeking work travel only if there is work. They would not persist at such cost and in the face of such grave dangers unless they were confident that their work was indeed needed. In a land where few will help and all seem hostile, the price of failing to find work can be self-destruction. Despite the tabloid press, baying for the blood of those who 'sponge' off the welfare system, illegal immigrants do not undertake the risks of migration for such a pathetic ambition. They want to work, and work hard, in order to earn as much as they can in a land that no doubt many of them loathe. They work at jobs the natives will no longer do: the dirty; the dangerous; the difficult. In doing so, they make possible better-paid employment for the natives. They buy food, use transport, find a place to stay – much of it to the benefit of natives. Their labour is necessary and they are eager to work. They accordingly contribute to the prosperity of the country in which they arrive, as well as helping their families and the places they come from: educating brothers and sisters; buying a plough or a washing machine; raising the money to marry. Why is this ambition criminal? If governments could indeed stop the migrants, it would be to the detriment of their own economies and therefore the quality of life for the inhabitants.

Such considerations at present weigh little in official calculations. Borders are more intensely patrolled, at growing cost, and punishments are increasingly draconian. Perhaps all these obstacles are really a secret test to sift out the weak? Only the fittest, the toughest and best equipped get through. Is it this that explains the militarisation of borders, the construction of fortifications in the style of the frontiers of the old Soviet Union (the fact that one was designed to keep people in, the other to keep them out, matters little), the conversion of those seeking work into criminal targets of manhunts and sniffer dogs? But this would suggest a greater capacity to plan carefully and secretly than is within the scope of most governments.

Furthermore, none of this touches on the worst aspect of the official obsession with preventing people crossing borders in search of work. Its most cruel effect is in destroying – or powerfully qualifying – the right to asylum. Victims fleeing persecution in their homelands are turned into 'illegal immigrants' in the country to which they turn for safety. So draconian has the regime of control become, it is ever more difficult even to enter a country legally in order to plead for sanctuary. The right to asylum, to some small measure of compassion, has become swamped in the hostility towards those who seek work. To deter those who want to work from pretending they are refugees, the regime governing asylum has to be as cruel as possible – including denying refugees the right to work and then bitterly complaining at the inevitable result of having to feed and house them. The refugees are forced to 'sponge' or to beg if they are to obey the law. The level of feeding and housing is lowered to the point at which no one would choose such an option except those driven by the most desperate necessity, by a terror of being destroyed.

Yet the problem of the jobs the natives will not do remains and will get worse. Native workers in developed countries are steadily better educated. As a result, the number of jobs they will not do increases. The decline in the birth rate in Japan, North America and Europe will sharply cut the number of workers available at precisely the time when the need for such workers will grow, particularly in light of the need to care for increasing numbers of aged citizens. Thus, the issue of immigration controls is closely bound up with the prospects of a secure and well-cared-for elderly generation.

These considerations are still remote from the immediate pre-occupations of government. The old xenophobia still has the power to win votes in election contests between parties. Enough people are willing to be taken for a ride, taken for suckers on the xenophobic ticket, to give politicians an interest in keeping immigration on the agenda. The experience of German xenophobia in the period of Naziism is not enough of a deterrent, and it still poses a major and irrational obstacle to the progress of the world. Appendix I describes a case of the manipulation of xenophobia in Britain on the issue of asylum-seeking.

Immigration controls

The increasingly heavy policing of the borders of North America and the EU is there to prevent only a certain class of people entering. The many casualties are drawn exclusively from that class, 'the unskilled'.

Casualties do not persuade the authorities against the use of controls. Governments have a responsibility to be hard-headed or 'tough-minded'. By this it is implied that sentimentality or moral qualms should not be allowed to cloud a clear perception of the national interest, lest governments betray their proper responsibility to protect their own citizens first and foremost. No matter how many misguided people seek to cross borders without the legal right to do so or, more commonly, overstay their visas or work when their visa forbids it, governments believe that unrestricted immigration is contrary to the social and economic interests of their population. They see immigrants as a cause of racism and xeno-phobia which, in turn, produce political instability. Citizens perceive immigrants to be stealing the jobs held by the natives by undercutting local wage levels, accepting levels of pay that the natives will not accept, accepting intolerable conditions of work and competing for scarce public services.

How valid are the fears of governments and of citizens? The bulk of this book sets out to explore this. It demonstrates that the evidence does not support these conclusions. More commonly, immigration expands the economy, creating more jobs and higher incomes for the natives. Indeed, such are the current trends that controls on immigration will increasingly undermine the welfare and the social and economic prospects of the people of developed countries. Immigration controls are becoming ever more economically destructive and socially senseless. On the other hand, governments fear that immigration undermines their sovereign powers, even if it does improve the economic welfare of the citizens – they are willing to sacrifice the second to maintain the first.

The following two chapters describe the context of controls. Chapter 2 documents how the present system of controls came about only in the twentieth century, particularly in the 1960s and 1970s. Before that time, there was general freedom for people to migrate, work and settle where they wished without government hindrance. Chapter 3 investigates the radically changed world context of controls in an increasingly integrated global economy. The incomes of people in the developed countries now depend upon this world system, on increasingly rapid free flows of trade and capital. Global networks are tending to supersede the old order of separate national economies. This would suggest that workers would also be increasingly mobile, and indeed many of them are. Immigration controls, however, severely limit this movement for the masses and result in a kind of global apartheid, with the majority of people legally disempowered from moving about the world.

Furthermore, maintaining controls threatens the occasionally large numbers of people fleeing natural or political disasters, locking them up with the danger, as it were. In trying to stop this movement, governments have extended controls from their own countries to the high seas, to airline carriers, and finally to the countries from which the refugees come, seeking to make escape from catastrophe impossible and contradicting the promises made to help those in flight.

At the same time, many classes of skilled and professional workers are able to move freely. So, in effect, controls are directed only at the majority of relatively unskilled, who, like medieval serfs, are supposed to be tied forever to the soil on which they were born, where their feudal obligations to the state are to be performed. As a result, those who most energetically seek work and incomes have to do so illegally. They slip out of the normal regulated conditions of work and living and are forced to live and work in conditions which are intolerable. The difference between those who are just looking for work and those who are traded internationally as slaves, women and children trafficked by criminals, grows blurred.

Chapter 4 examines the arguments advanced for the control of immigration – that without controls immigrants will swamp developed countries, producing a violent, racist and xenophobic reaction; that they will steal the jobs of the natives, force down wages and that consequently conditions will deteriorate. There is the notion that immigrants destroy a nation and the cultural identities of its people; or that immigrants will crowd out the natives in access to public services and housing, resulting in aggravated social problems: segregation, lack of assimilation, increasing costs of and falling standards in education, increased crime.

Chapter 5 details some of the reasons why we need to end controls, giving evidence of the severe need in developed countries for unskilled workers, without whom native unemployment among the skilled will increase. It argues that controls do not work. So great is the need for unskilled workers, so faulty any politically acceptable regime of control, that illegal immigration will necessarily increase, and when the immigrant communities reach significant proportions, governments will be forced to recognise reality and offer periodic amnesties. We look at the manner in which immigration has historically revitalised cultures and stimulated economies, expanding job prospects and incomes for natives. The controls imposed force people to settle, and without them many more people would circulate between a homeland and a country in which to work, thereby sending cash or carrying home skills and knowledge to develop their home economies. The progress of the developing countries becomes much more possible when immigration controls are lifted. Since the debate about immigration controls, now coupled with asylum-seeking, is one of the biggest sources of racism and xenophobia, ending controls will remove one of the main sources.

Chapter 6 looks then at the current situation, in which the old system of immigration controls, set up in the 1960s and 1970s, is beginning to crumble and asks why this is so. It explores the changes facilitated by the sudden outbreak of competition among developed countries to capture a share of the world's supply of skilled workers, particularly in IT. But this is only one factor forcing change. The growing number of elderly in developed countries is beginning to increase the demand for labour-intensive services, particularly in the caring professions, at precisely a time when the number of workers is set to decline drastically. It will therefore become impossibly expensive for the elderly to buy a secure and decent old age, particularly for the poorest. Furthermore tradeable services are becoming the engine of growth in the world economy. Developed countries want to expand the outlets for their services – banking, insurance, transport, IT – which means service-providers from developed countries have to be allowed to migrate, to live and work in developing countries. However, this cannot be a one-way process, and developing countries will only allow it if their workers are allowed the same privilege in developed countries.

The final chapter returns to the themes of global integration and the mobility of workers. Following the model of the liberalisation of trade, governments need now to begin to go through sets of negotiations for the mutual reduction in restrictions to migration, to free labour. In doing so, they will remove the distinction between legal and illegal migration. Once clandestine movement is ended, it becomes possible to regulate both the conditions of migration and of work. Furthermore, it means police efforts, at present squandered on detecting and deporting people looking for work, can be focussed on the real problem, trafficking in women and children, in slaves. Similarly, if asylum-seekers are allowed to work as soon as they arrive, they will no longer be a burden on public expenditure and hence a source of xenophobia. Resources can then be concentrated on those refugees who cannot work: the aged, the disabled, the young mothers and so forth. But above all, the removal of controls will allow the people of the developing countries to work. The results will be both secure care for the aged of the developed countries and the acceleration of the development of the developing world.

1 — Movement

How has the existing pattern of immigration controls come about?

For much of human history, movement – migration – has been the norm: an endless search for new hunting grounds, new pastures, new sources of goods to be traded, new means of work. The rise of the modern national state changed that. Territories were fenced and policed. Trade and people were required to cross taxing and control points. Movement continued, but now with more difficulty.

Until quite recently, however, many rulers welcomed newcomers as additional workers, soldiers and taxpayers, as pioneers with energy and initiative, adding to the power of the ruler. Many, in the same spirit, tried to prevent emigration, especially of skilled workers, as a loss of their power.

With the modern state came the spread of capitalism, the market economy, a much more dynamic system that was continually opening new areas, transforming old ones. Movement – from where people lived to where, on farm, in mine or factory, they could work – became intrinsic to the system. Migration became vital for the continued growth of the world's output, the growth in incomes. Of course, most of the movement was not between countries, but to the local town or city, to different regions in the same country, to the emerging giant industrial cities. For many, then as now, migration was a part of the normal life-cycle, whether for a season to harvest crops or work on building sites, for long enough to save to build a house and home, to marry or put a child through education, or for much of a working life, or for ever.

Yet even so there were major international movements. Between 10 and 20 million people were lifted by force out of Africa over a

200-year period – with enormous losses and cruelties – to man the emerging plantations of sugar and tobacco in North and South America. From 1840 to 1930, around 50 million Indians and Chinese went to California, South-east Asia, the Caribbean and Africa to build railways and cities, to farm and mine gold. By 1930, there were some 30 million Indians working abroad, of whom in the region of 24 million ultimately returned to India. The great mines of the Rand sucked in thousands of workers from Central and Eastern Africa. And between 1800 and 1930, in the region of 60 or 70 million Europeans moved to the Americas, to parts of Africa, to Australia and New Zealand.

These were some of the more dramatic long-distance movements to newly opened areas. But within smaller areas masses of people moved to work, especially within Europe during the headlong growth of industry in the nineteenth century. British development depended heavily on the continuous arrival of new generations of workers from Ireland and elsewhere. The French drew in Belgians, Italians, Poles and Spaniards. Belgium recruited Italians. Germany drew heavily on Poles and others from Eastern Europe. And in the gigantic boom of the Second World War, Germany forced eight million workers into the country. The faster the economy grew, the greater the movement.

Within countries, workers moved – to the Ruhr, to northern Italy (from the south), to the industrial north of Britain; and in the US, people concentrated in the north-east (New York to Boston to Philadelphia), then the north-centre (Chicago and the Lakes), then California and now in the south. The dynamism of the economy constantly transformed the geography, reshuffling workers and so population.

The rise of the modern state

However, parallel to this major movement of people was the spread of a new kind of state, of nationalism, and of what we have called 'the fencing of territory', a change which radically altered the terms and hence the patterns of worker movement. Governments set out more or less consciously to standardise the population under their rule, to make nations out of the collection of clans, tribes and families that inhabited the land the rulers controlled. This was done by means of standard language and laws, a common educational system, a territory integrated internally through roads and later railways. In some cases, a common religion was enforced and those minorities that did not accept it were isolated or expelled. The success of the process was in establishing the unchallenged authority of government, a willingness of the population to pay for government, and, in the event of war, fight for it – national conscription was a powerful means to force standardisation. Ultimately, people could hardly comprehend a world not fenced in national patches, a population not divided into clear and exclusive nationalities.

By implication, the norm was now not migration but permanent settlement. The inhabitants of a country were supposed to be immobile, and to have been so for time immemorial. Some argued that the nations of Europe were not new inventions but as ancient as humanity itself, that the lands occupied had been held for millennia, that cultures were distinctive and descended from ancient times. Of course, any half-decent historian could show the claims were nonsense. Few modern nations could claim continuity for more than a few hundred years, let alone in the same place. Indeed, the distinctive peoples of the Europe of a millennium-and-a-half ago have long since disappeared – Normans, Vikings, Franks, Goths, Huns and so on.

In the past two centuries, the system was not only created, but extended to every part of the globe. The social and cultural fault lines were redrawn between the newly invented countries. The state took over that zealous hatred of outsiders – as with a hypersensitive sense of collective honour and egotism – that used to govern villages, tribes and extended families in the past. Loyalty to the state and a hatred of foreigners seemed two sides of the same coin. War raised these issues to a peak, but xenophobia in mild or moderate forms became functional to the system. What a medieval merchant, say, would have taken for granted – the peaceful co-existence of different 'nations' living in the same city – and what had been repeated in the twentieth century in such cosmopolitan centres as Alexandria, Shanghai and Singapore, or imperial capitals such as Vienna, became threatening and dangerous.

However, until the twentieth century, controls over the movement of people, with some exceptions, remained relatively lax
(exceptions include tsarist Russia, Prussia, imperial China and
Japan). It was fortunate, since this allowed the large-scale movement
of refugees driven out precisely by the attempts of governments
to enforce a social or religious uniformity on their peoples – as
with the expulsion of Jews from Spain and tsarist Russia, of the
Huguenot Protestants from France, of the Armenians from Turkey,
and of the appalling endless savageries inflicted on the former
citizens of the Austro – Hungarian empire in the Balkans, and,
finally, the holocaust in Nazi Germany. On the other hand, the great
powers used their newly 'homogenised' populations to extend
their global power, through colonising new territories.

While 'ethnic cleansing' continued in the twentieth century,
those in flight now collided with formal barriers – the Jews of
Germany like the Roma of Eastern Europe found homes only with
great difficulty. In the past, it was easier to move, as the economic
need for workers took precedence over any political aim to impose
a social uniformity on the population.

In the twentieth century, the fences became great walls to regulate
the arrival of newcomers, now seen not as an acquisition of strength
but as the infiltration of enemies. Indeed, in the heyday of empire
the great powers encouraged emigration as a means to extend
political influence and trade. For most people, migration between
countries was coming to be seen as rare, exceptional, almost an act of
disloyalty. Of course, movement there had to be – even if officially
abnormal – if wealth and hence the power of government was
to grow. Wars were a time not only when governments demanded
the greatest acts of loyalty from their citizens, but also when maps
were redrawn and populations found themselves living under
governments which rejected them. After World War II, 25–30 million
people found themselves disinherited and moved west or south. The
partition of India led to some 16 million moving between the two
new countries. Furthermore, there were regular bouts of ethnic
cleansing to carve out new states in Palestine, South-east Asia and
Sub-Saharan Africa.

Thus, the search for work increasingly collided with the
imperatives of governments to segregate their populations, or rather

it led to contradictory impulses – an economic drive to recruit workers if they were ever needed to sustain economic growth, but a social and political drive to exclude foreigners and 'purify' the population as an instrument of power.

After 1945: Europe

After the Second World War, Western Europe and Japan experienced a reconstruction boom which led on to rapid growth to catch up with the US. This resulted in an extraordinary period of economic expansion for two-and-a-half decades. The US itself, having boomed during the war, stagnated for a long period before also sharing the growth. Japan and the US fuelled growth in East and then South-east Asia, and Latin America. The economic geography of the world was subject to more dramatic changes than ever before.

In the period between the world wars (1918–39), the Great Depression and economic stagnation meant that few jobs were created (indeed, there was long-term mass unemployment) so there was relatively little migration. Only France, after the terrible losses of the First War, continued to recruit. Elsewhere, controls on movement were effective only because workers were little needed. Indeed, some states (such as the Soviet Union) could impose closure, an end to significant immigration or emigration, in the interests of political domination.

With a European boom after 1947, economic regulations – including the control of migration – increasingly restricted economic growth. There was increasing pressure to decontrol. Germany had the good luck to get an immense inflow of refugees from Eastern Europe, especially from the newly independent communist state of East Germany (until the Berlin Wall was built to lock the citizens in). Britain started reconstruction after the war by recruiting workers from Eastern Europe. But still, by the mid-1950s, there were clear signs of a growing shortage of workers throughout Western Europe. Agriculture was everywhere being stripped of its workers to man urban industry, and later women were drawn from, or driven out of, the home and into work. Those who made things which needed a lot of workers – garments or shoes, for example – began for the first time to buy these outside Europe, in low-wage areas (especially at that time from Hong Kong). Later, they set up factories there and in North Africa, Eastern Europe and then, South-east Asia, and themselves exported to Europe and now North America. In addition, there were hundreds of thousands of new exporters in the developing countries.

All this was done but was not enough. Germany and France, the miracle economies, began to recruit workers in Southern Italy and Spain. Britain shipped workers from its former empire; India, the Caribbean, West Africa. It was still not enough – particularly when the Italian economy also began to expand rapidly, attracting its workers home. The German government moved on to recruit in Greece, what was then Yugoslavia, Turkey and Iran. The French relied on their former ex-colonies in North Africa, and on Spain and Portugal. The areas from which workers were now being recruited far exceeded anything in the past, going beyond the boundaries not only of the national territory but also of Europe itself.

The German government tried to limit the effect by drawing a sharp line between those in Germany temporarily for work, *gastarbeiter*, and those who were Germans, permanently settled. It did not work. The competition between employers to find and hold workers forced them to offer increasingly more attractive terms – rights to housing, to medical benefits, to bring a family into Germany. The government might hold out against granting citizenship, even to those born in Germany, but the practical differences between citizen and immigrant worker grew steadily blurred.

The new workers were often put to work in farming (to make up for those who had moved to the cities) and construction. As the economy changed, native workers moved on to factories and offices, to better-paid jobs, and the migrants replaced them. Finally, many native workers left the factories and immigrants took their places. The newcomers made it possible for the native workers or their children, with steadily higher educational qualifications, to escape to better-paid and cleaner jobs.

By the early 1970s, France and Germany each had about two-and-a-half-million foreigners in their workforces, with a possible eleven-and-a-half million in Europe as a whole (excluding foreign-born 'ethnic Germans' from Eastern Europe, admitted to settle as citizens in Germany). By then, almost simultaneously, the European powers were moving to tighten control on entries. The British, facing an influx of Asians holding British passports from East Africa, imposed the first controls in 1962. A little later, the French moved to regulate entries. By the time of the onset of the worst world recession since the Second World War, in 1973, much of Western Europe had imposed controls. Having actively pursued immigration, Europe now moved to end it – or rather, to end specific flows: Asians, Africans and Caribbeans into Britain, Turks into Germany, Arabs and Africans into France.

Furthermore, at various times, governments tried to force immigrants already in the country to leave. In the case of Germany, 'immigrants' included the children of immigrant parents even if they were born and raised in Germany, so their 'repatriation' was in fact exile. There were campaigns of intimidation, including notorious street checks by police. Some governments offered direct payments to persuade people to go; others were deported. The efforts were sporadic, feverish and frequently deceitful. Like the debate about immigration controls, they did much to increase racial prejudice and give public respectability to racial discrimination. Efforts were made to prevent the reunification of families, to block the arrival of children, and to prevent marriages that involved immigration. Often the legal basis for this did not exist, so it was pursued only in the confidentiality of the offices of European consulates issuing visas abroad.

In the 45 years to 1995, there had been 28 million arrivals and 20 million departures. The net addition to the European population was 13 million, including children born in Europe. Tables 1 and 2 (see Tables and Figures section) show the different shares of these between countries.

However, some new immigration of workers did continue, in addition to which the reunification of families was generally allowed. In Britain, as mentioned earlier, the Irish continued to enter the country freely up to 1992, when EU changes allowed free migration for all EU citizens, including the Irish. Germany continued to admit 'ethnic Germans', those who though born abroad could prove German descent (usually from Eastern Europe and the ex-Soviet Union). Some countries admitted specialised professionals.

Under this heading, the national origin of people entering Britain for work in 1997 was thus: 18 per cent from the US; 11 per cent Australian; 6 per cent South African; 5 per cent New Zealander; 3 per cent Canadian; 2 per cent Polish (see Table 3 in the Tables and Figures section). Some of these immigrants may have been black or brown, but it is reasonable to assume that they would be predominantly white – this exception appeared to have been used in a racially discriminatory way. About 16 per cent were non-white – 7 per cent Indian; 4 per cent Japanese; 4 per cent Pakistani; 3 per cent Filipino. In addition, different countries allowed different numbers of workers (as opposed to non-workers) in immigration – Figure 1 (in the Tables and Figures section) shows that Britain and Switzerland selected about half their immigrants on their status as workers, compared – at this stage – to 2 per cent for the US.

America and immigration

North America did not have the same experience as Europe. There was no post-war reconstruction boom, and the economy was notorious for its weakness in the 1950s and much of the 1960s. But it still needed workers in some sectors. Up to then, the Braceros programme allowed Mexican farm labourers to enter. From the mid-1960s, this began to change, particularly in view of the two phases of rapid growth in the 1980s and, especially, 1990s. The number of immigrants overtook the first great surge of growth before the First World War. Between 1901 and 1910, around eight-and-a-half million migrants landed in the US, equal to about 15 per cent of the population then. In the 1990s, nearly 12 million (8.8 million legal and, at a guess, 2.8 million illegal); that was 10 per cent of a much larger population.

As in Europe, the immigrants were younger than the natives, concentrated in the age range between 20 and 40. As a result, they were a much larger share of the growth in the workforce – a quarter in the decade of the 1990s, fully half in some years. In the border states of Texas and California, home to many of the immigrants, they were as important as natives in the growth of the workforce. In the medium-term projection for the US population – to reach 387 million in 2050 – 80 million of the 124 million total increase arises from immigration.

The US government does not record who leaves the country, emigration, yet it has always been important. Depending on how easy and cheap transport was, many chose to work in the US for only part of their lives. Many Mexican illegal immigrants only want a job for a season, and then prefer to head home. It is notorious that of the great numbers entering the country in the first decade-and-a-half of the twentieth century, up to 40 per cent returned home. Perhaps 300,000 people a year emigrate from the US, equal to between 35 and 45 per cent of those who immigrate. In Europe the figures fluctuate, but, for example, Germany had more people leaving in 1997 than entering, as Britain has done in most years since 1945.

Economies are continually changing, and governments' attitudes towards immigration reflect this. So the law and regulations have to be constantly adjusted. Take Appendix II, a thumbnail sketch of American legislation. It begins with open borders and no legislation, proceeds through racial exclusions (Chinese and Japanese), to a fully fledged quota system to try to reproduce some historical US nation, whether of 1890 or 1910 – cloning the American 'race'. Cloning was not scrapped until 1965, when family reunification was to take 80 per cent of the immigrant visa quota. Now emerging as a parallel trend is the recruitment of those skilled and professional workers the government, spurred by employers, thinks are needed. This is being implemented simultaneously with increasing attempts to control illegal entries, to stop unskilled workers entering. Appendix II shows just how complicated the admissions process has become, and it still does not achieve what is intended – the admission of those who are wanted and the exclusion of the rest.

In both North America and Europe, immigration and refugee arrivals have immensely increased the number of different places from which people originate. Immigrants and refugees head for where they are most likely to get work, so they are heavily concentrated in particular regions and cities. In the US, six states get the bulk of foreigners – California, New York, Texas, Florida, New Jersey and Illinois. Texas and California house around 40 per cent between them. In these six states, 93 per cent of foreigners head for the biggest cities. By 1960, 46 per cent of Miami's citizens were foreign-born, a third of Los Angeles's. Table 4 shows something of the diversity of origins in Asia. This concentration produces a dramatic cosmopolitanism in the largest cities of North America and Europe, almost little UNs in themselves. Some schools in Los Angeles claim they have children speaking well over a hundred different languages, while the Mayor of Dade, Miami, claims 156 nationalities in his city. White Hart Lane School in north London claims 55 languages.

The changing demand for workers in the US determines the changing type, skill and gender of the immigrant workers who offer themselves for hire. Immigrant workers are bunched at each end of the range of skills – unskilled labour or professional and highly skilled. Twelve-and-and-half per cent of America's immigrants in the 1990s had graduate degrees, compared to 10 per cent of Americans. Thirty per cent of immigrant men did not have the equivalent of a highschool diploma, compared to under 10 per cent of Americans. This was the result of a faster increase in educational qualifications in the US than the countries from which immigrants came, particularly Mexico. In 1960, 54 per cent of American men did not have a high-school diploma, compared to 70 per cent of the foreign-born population. Nonetheless, in comparison to immigrants before the First World War, ancestors of many modern Americans, these standards are a vast improvement – as previously the lion's share of the immigrants would have been illiterate.

At the same time, incomes of Americans are increasingly unequal, with a decline in income for the lowest-paid 10 per cent of the population. It is here that many of the immigrants are concentrated. In the 1990s, the lowest-paid group of foreign-born workers, Mexicans, had incomes 40 per cent below the native equivalent in unskilled work. The gap narrows the longer they stay in America, but to reach parity can take between 16 and 20 years.

The world

The number of people settled outside their home country actually remains very small. It is perhaps 200 million, having risen from an estimate of 75 million in 1965 and 120 million in 1990. About 48 per cent worldwide, but over half of immigrants to Europe and North

America are said to be women. Illegal immigrants – 'undocumented', 'clandestine', 'irregular' – may double the numbers. But this is still a tiny proportion of the world's 6 billion people (something under 7 per cent). International migration is thus quite rare. But because where migrants come from and go to is highly concentrated, the number seems much bigger in particular localities. Domestic migration would immensely increase the figure.

More remarkable than any increase in immigrant numbers in the last quarter of the twentieth century is the increase in sources and destinations. Economic growth has spread to much of the world, sooner or later creating new flows wherever growth develops. We can see the dim outlines of a world labour market emerging even though much of it is clandestine. Consider South Korea and its breakneck process of economic development. In a generation, the country has come from backwardness to being relatively advanced. This has not stopped emigration. You can see its results in the hundreds of Korean corner delicatessens and restaurants in Buenos Aires and Santiago de Chile, New York and London. Korea's garment factories are largely manned by illegal Chinese immigrants. Similar examples are found worldwide: the little Punjabi supermarkets in Oslo, the Iranian building workers in north Tokyo, the Thai women who staff Taiwan's industrial estates, the Filipinas who run the stores of Bahrain's free zone, the Afghans, Somalis and Ethiopians who drive Washington's taxis; all this without mentioning the instant cosmopolitan workforces who make possible the extraction of oil in the Gulf – by 1990, 60 per cent of Kuwait's population was foreign-born. In the world network of major cities, the sinews of the new global economy are already being operated by a global workforce.

2 — Wrestling with the Hydra

A global economy

A world of national economies as described in the last chapter has, however, been overtaken by new patterns of integration. As a result, the migration system founded upon that system of national units is increasingly undermined and outdated.

The world is in transition – from a set of relatively separate national economies to an integrated single global economy. We are as yet far from the final outcome, but already what is called 'globalisation' indicates the trend. In such a world, places in many different countries collaborate to produce the world's output of goods and services. The process is fuelled by capital flows from around the world – without, as it were, nationality. In an open world economy, the world's workers would also be more mobile. For each government, increasingly its income and the prosperity of its people depend upon facilitating that movement, regardless of where people choose to settle or live.

Not all governments publish figures on the movement of people in and out of their country, so it is difficult to show increasing mobility. However, the US produced estimates of 'non-immigrant arrivals' from 1994 to 1996 (see Table 5). In 1996 (the last year for which figures are available) there were just under 25 million of these. The bulk, 19 million, were 'temporary visitors for pleasure' or tourists (rising from 7 million in 1980). However, a faster-growing group of entrants came in the form of 'temporary workers' (18.6

per cent up, compared to 12 per cent for all non-immigrant entrants), including transfers of staff within companies (43 per cent up), followed by 'professionals for temporary work' (36.5 per cent up). The period is too short to draw hard conclusions, but even so, the changes in movement are quite large. Furthermore, it is from these groups – tourists and temporary workers – that many of the illegal immigrants come: people who overstay the limit on their visas, or in the case of tourists, people who flout the condition of their tourist visa by taking a job. More surprising is that in these years, when the American economy was already growing fast, the temporary worker group did not include more unskilled or agricultural workers; both groups declined in these years (by 27.4 per cent for agricultural workers, by 8.9 per cent for non-agricultural workers). Other types of visa entry did not make this up – so that inevitably illegal movement took the strain (The INS estimates the annual illegal inflow at this time as 200–300,000 annually). Student admissions remained important and many students subsequently became immigrants.

Increasing international movement of workers collides with the attempts to control movement, to, as it were, immobilise the bulk of the world's population. The attempt to control entry to their countries leads the governments of the developed nations to seek to control the world at large, to control people leaving their countries and travelling to Europe or North America.

Building the fortress

In the 1990s, governments were not yet trying to make up in immigration what was lacking in their domestic workforce, let alone distinguishing more between the right to work and the right to settle. They were mainly shoring up their defences, making controls on the entry of settlers ever more tight. In doing so, they were creating and sustaining an ever larger black economy and a new source of popular paranoid fantasy, the illegal immigrant.

It was a paradox that this occurred in the midst of rejoicing at the collapse of the Soviet Union and its former Eastern European allies. This entailed the dismantling of some of the most ferocious structures of border control, symbolised by the wall slicing Berlin in half. The borders had been famous lines of tyranny across Europe – high fences and trenches leaping across the hills, thickets of barbed wire and minefields, punctuated by watch towers, with machine guns and spot-lights, helicopters clattering day and night along the length. Above all, the mighty fortifications represented a will to kill all who might stray near, let alone seek to cross. Yet in these very years the US and European governments were constructing just such fortifications on their outer borders – the 'tortilla curtain', the aluminium version of the Iron Curtain dividing communist and non-communist Europe – this time between the US and Mexico. In 1998, the EU approved the cash to build a fence across its southernmost border in Spanish Ceuta next to Morocco. Algerian President Abdelaziz Bouteflika watched, he said, the construction of a new Great Wall of China to exclude its neighbours. It was humbug to say that the purpose of the one was to lock people in, of the other to lock them out, for the effect was identical. The control of migration had come to be seen not as an economic question but as one of security, of crime, a threat to democracy and civil society. The bedraggled Mexican tomato picker, the Albanian street seller, the Senegalese cleaner, were cast in the heroic role of invading warriors. The hostility towards foreigners so thoroughly inculcated in populations was now focussed on the poorest and most defenceless of the world's workers.

In fact, border fortifications were, despite the rapidly rising cost, slightly shadow-play. Illegal immigrants were more likely to be people who entered legally but stayed on or worked illegally. But the drama of the borders, of border chases and checks, of smugglers and stowaways, captured the popular imagination and awakened ancient paranoid fantasies of invasion. The excitement of the hunt neutralised any compassion for the pathetic hunted.

Yet even on the southern border of the US, even with – as Dunn (1996) describes it – the militarisation of parts of the border, there was only a 30 per cent chance of being caught entering the country without the right papers. There was only a 1–2 per cent chance of being arrested once you had entered the country illegally. The dangers grew substantially with the increasing fortification of the border. Controlling the most frequently used crossing points forced migrants into the more remote and dangerous areas, the deserts and mountains of Arizona and New Mexico, or fast-flowing rivers. The danger of death or disability rose accordingly.

In Europe, migration was a police matter, and illegal migration was seen as crime, in the same file as forced labour, trafficking, prostitution, smuggling narcotics. It was as if parking offences were classified in the same category as killing pedestrians and all road crimes. Just as the American campaign to ban alcohol in the inter-war Prohibition era was so effective in creating and sustaining the Mafia, so the policing of borders in Europe creates and sustains the gangs that organise illegal movement across borders. Furthermore, as many of the workers moving – from Iraq, China, Pakistan, India, Nigeria and so on – were physically distinguished, rigorous policing was inevitably racist. The wrong skin colour, physical build, foreign accent or 'alien' behaviour was automatically a cause for suspicion, surveillance and interception.

There was always a danger that a vigilant popular press might, in dramatic pictures of the brutality on the border, reverse the tide and turn anger to pity. Increasing efforts were made to ensure it was impossible even to reach the border and the press photographers. In the US, the coastguards tried to stop people reaching the Florida beaches, so they could not qualify to sue for the right to stay. In the 1980s, 20,000 seaborne Haitians were prevented from landing, their boats turned back to the open sea (the British reproached Washington on this when the US government protested at the then British Hong Kong forcibly expelling Vietnamese boatpeople – see Appendix III). In November 1999, in a famous case, a Cuban boat capsized in similar circumstances, drowning ten of those aboard, including the mother and step father of a small boy, Elian González; he became a *cause célèbre* in the tussle between those trying to keep him in the US and those, including the US government, insisting he be returned to his Cuban father. It was strange that so much fuss should have been made about the small boy, so little about the drowning of the other ten.

In Europe, the attempt to prevent people arriving took several forms. One was helping neighbours to fortify their borders – Germany helped Poland fortify its eastern border with Russian Kaliningrad, Lithuania, Belarus and the Ukraine. EU subsidies went to Morocco to fund fortification of its borders and increase the interception of migrants. Morocco complained at the burden of policing for Europe (17,178 were expelled in 1998; since many had journeyed far to try to reach Spain, they merely tried again). The US helped Mexico strengthen the defences of its southern borders with Guatemala.

Policing was extended to the high seas, flouting existing rights of freedom to travel. US coastguards intercepted at sea Chinese ships, diverting them to Mexico or the Caribbean. The Italians patrolled the Mediterranean. The Australians guarded the northern sea lanes to intercept and turn back Indonesian boats carrying Chinese, Afghans and Iraqis.

Many governments tried to punish those who transported migrants without proper documents – airlines, shipping companies, truck drivers – a system of 'carrier liability'. For example, Britain fined airlines £30.7 million between 1987 and 1991 for carrying migrants with defective documents (the airlines had the additional costs of taking the migrants back again). The fine for carrying migrants across the Channel in trucks was levied at double what the fare was thought to be (£2,000). Some carriers were caught on the other side – in October 1977, three shipping companies were charged with racial discrimination by the French police for refusing to issue tickets to cross the Channel to asylum-seekers from the Czech and Slovak Republics. Other shipowners evaded risks by dumping stowaways overboard.

To ease some of the problems airlines had in checking travel documents, the EU in October 1996 urged member governments to appoint immigration staff as airline liaison officers in foreign airports. By 1999, the British had 20 of these, working usually in collaboration with the local governments. In effect they were trying to prevent people fleeing the country, a right guaranteed under the UN Declaration of Human Rights. Seeking to end illegal immigration had now become a policy of preventing people escaping persecution.

The European governments also agreed that the government of the territory where a migrant first landed was obliged to take them back. Fleeing from Bosnia by land necessarily meant crossing Croatia, so regardless of where the person finally arrived, they could be returned by force to that country – 'an obscene game of pass-the-parcel,' as Edward Mortimer of the *Financial Times* (9

December 1992) called it. It was also a strong signal to Croatia not to accept the entry of anyone who might move on and claim later to be a refugee. The same followed from a hundred or more re-admission treaties that governments signed with countries from which migrants had immediately come, permitting people to be returned by force. This allowed a Sri Lankan arriving in Germany from Poland to be returned to Poland, and then deported to wherever the migrant had come from, and so on, back to Sri Lanka. The bribe of aid was used with 71 of the world's governments to induce them to accept people deported from Europe even if they did not live in that country.

If people could not be prevented from fleeing – from, say, civil wars in Sri Lanka, Somalia, Rwanda or Yugoslavia – efforts were bent to keeping them near their original home so they would not reach Europe. Iraqi Kurds must either stay in the 'safe haven' of northern Iraq or be diverted to Turkey (with its notorious record on the treatment of Kurds) or Jordan. Similar provisions were developed for Sri Lanka, Afghanistan and Somalia. The Turkish government, accused widely of the abuse of human rights and the torture of prisoners, in this way became a partner with European governments in frustrating both migration to Europe and the right to flee.

There was also much talk about establishing tolerable regimes in the countries from which migrants came, so that they were not obliged to flee. This was hypocrisy, because Western governments have little power to shape the human-rights regimes in other countries. Efforts were made to steer aid programmes to discourage emigration, but these were equally futile. Aid was tiny in the sum of things and could not start the scale of boom likely to influence migration. Nevertheless it seemed to be doing something – a British Conservative MEP rejoiced in his scheme – an 'excellent use of taxpayers' money. Instead of spending £200 on a hostel for a single refugee in Britain, the same money will put many more people back on their feet – in their own homes and on their own land.' What? In a civil war?

Refugee policy had been created by the Western powers simply as a reproach to the old Soviet Union and its allies during the Cold War. The collapse of those regimes removed the whole justification. The right to emigrate which had become enshrined in international law was now more or less deliberately subverted. Indeed, some Western governments considered making it a criminal offence to leave a country without 'proper documentation'. If achieved, this would end the right to flee persecution or the threat of death. Refugees had become simply illegal migrants.

Thus, attempts to prevent entry of unskilled workers led to ever greater efforts to control international travel and departures from sending countries, to control world movement. In the midst of supposed universal liberalisation, policy for the majority of the world's population developed in exactly the opposite direction: to increased control.

Domestic controls

Governments found it almost impossible to trace illegal immigrants once they were in the country, but they tried. Sometimes, travellers were subjected to random police checks on the Metro in Paris and on the streets of London. They could not fail to be racially discriminatory, and were very unpopular, particularly among the young who were most often the targets. Checks were instituted through various state agencies – social security and health offices, schools for new children. Occasionally, places of work were subject to random checks. Both the French and American governments introduced penalties for employers who hired the undocumented, but they were difficult to administer. Employers, like airline counter officials, resented being forced to act as unpaid agents of immigration authorities. They could not be expected to do more than check the documents offered by people applying for jobs, but everyone knew forged documents were easily available (in November 1998, the INS seized two million fake identity papers in Los Angeles). The INS in the US could not expect to check more than a tiny proportion of the workplaces in the country. Furthermore, some of the illegal immigrants worked in the black economy, in unregistered workplaces. Again, it was polit- ically difficult. Workers, and increasingly trade unions and local neighbourhoods dependent on one main employer, resented the disorganisation of random checks of workplaces and the deportation of key workers. Ultimately, the detection rate was low and the cost high, both in terms of the INS workforce and local political support. Highway checks were even less fruitful – and more irritating as those selected to be checked would be chosen on racial grounds, but few would be guilty.

But tighter border controls did increase the dangers of the process. They also increased the costs – and the returns to the smugglers. Only the better-off could expect to raise the funds necessary to employ the professionals who could find the means to cross borders or defeat the controls at other entry points.

Meeting the demand for workers

Increasing controls, however, does not stop the demand for unskilled workers. Economic expansion, as we have noted, invariably increases the demand for workers beyond what is locally available. So does structural change in an economy, increasing the demand for some workers and decreasing that for others. The efforts of US and European governments to raise workers' educational standards only exaggerates the problems. For now workers refuse to do a mass of ill-paid, dirty and harsh jobs; understandably they demand – and their education seems to justify – better-paid jobs in good conditions. With tight immigration controls, rising educational standards alone create a great shortage of unskilled workers, even when there may be high unemployment. It is that gap which makes vital the migrant.

There are, as we have seen, ways of adjusting to the shortage. Food and drink dispensers can replace waitresses, drivers rather than special conductors collect bus fares. Other jobs can be sent abroad, as with the garment industry. Governments fortunate enough to have a pool of labour in a neighbouring country could allow daily cross-border commuting – from Poland, the Czech Republic and Slovakia, to Germany and Austria; from Mexico to the southern states of the US; from Malaysia to Singapore or China to Hong Kong. Another means is to permit greater use of contract workers – companies recruit workers wherever they are cheapest, employ them, usually on infrastructure and building projects, and remove them from the country when the job is done. The company is responsible and fined heavily if its workers do not leave. There were said to be 20 million such workers worldwide in the 1990s. Korean companies employed Filipinos and others for projects in the Persian Gulf or Saudi Arabia. Chinese companies used Chinese workers in the same way in projects in the Middle East and Africa. Thai and Filipino women operated factories in Taiwan, and Thai and Portugese workers were taken to Israel to replace expelled Palestinians.

There were other exceptions. As we have seen, often skilled workers had special privileges to enter countries. Temporary workers could also sometimes escape immigration rules. In 1995, the EU had nearly seven million of these, over a third of them women (for the official figures up to 1997, see Table 6). In Asia, the migration of women became very important – they accounted for 55 per cent of worker migration in 1973, 80 per cent in 1994. In 1998, women were four times more numerous than men in Indonesian emigration, and 64 per cent of Filipino emigration. Many of them went to work as maids, nannies and cooks in the Middle East and South-east Asia, but also to do factory jobs or work in entertainment, hotels, restaurants and the retail trade.

Particular countries had other exceptions. The British allowed in for work 'working holiday-makers', aged 17 to 27, from the old (white) Commonwealth (there were 23,200 in 1990; 33,300 in 1997). In 1997, over half were from Australia, a quarter from New Zealand and 7 per cent from Canada.

In countries with a significant farming industry, agriculture was always a problem. The number of workers needed for the harvest was often enormous. As we have seen, the US government, pressured by farming lobbies from states with intensive cultivation (fruit and vegetables), often made special provision for this task for seasonal migrants from Mexico, outside the normal immigration rules. The Braceros programme (1942–64) allowed at its peak half a million seasonal workers into the country. Some people believe this sharply reduced illegal migration, but others dispute it. Pressure from trade unions, church and civil rights groups ended the scheme. Without border controls, this circulation might persist indefinitely (a 1978 study of Mexican farm workers suggested that under a fifth expressed any interest in staying after the harvest), but the tighter controls increasingly forced workers into illegality – and increased the incentives for workers to settle in the US rather than face the hazards of crossing and recrossing the frontier. The government was forced to acknowledge the real state of affairs with the 1986 Immigration Control and Reform Act, which offered an amnesty to illegal entrants, with a special scheme for farm-workers. The farmer lobbies were afraid that giving workers an amnesty would mean that they would desert the land, so the amnesty was made dependent on workers continuing in farm work for three years (with a further two years needed to qualify for US citizenship). 1.8 million applied for the amnesty, with another 1.3 million under the special scheme for farm workers.

European farmers also faced increasing difficulties in recruiting workers as their children opted for city jobs. Germany's seasonal worker scheme brought in, mainly from Poland, some 226,000 workers for three months in 1997 (up from 154,500 in 1994). Left to themselves, German employers would probably have brought in many more workers – in October 1990, they applied for 70,289 workers, 98 per cent of them by name; the government granted permits for 800. At the same time, some German farmers were buying farms in western Poland and so escaping the tangles of German immigration laws (their American colleagues had long purchased land in Mexico through local nominees, again escaping border problems).

Italy faced growing problems in worker recruitment in the 1990s for jobs shunned by Italians in farming, tourism, construction, domestic service and home care. Workers from outside the EU increased sharply, and of the 25 per cent increase in the 1990s, 40 per cent were in agriculture.

The British also operate a scheme to admit seasonal farm workers, but it is limited to students, aged 18–25, who are allowed to enter for three months before 30 November of each year. The number was capped at 10,000, and in practice numbers rose from 3,600 in 1992 to 9,300 in 1997, 98 per cent from Eastern Europe (and 40 per cent from Poland). However, numbers were still below what farmers wanted. Four hundred students from Kiev University, Ukraine, applied for temporary work permits to do seasonal farming in Britain in 2000, but the annual allocation of 10,000 permits had been exhausted. The National Farmers' Union estimated that there was a 25 per cent shortfall in the number of workers available, which hit the soft-fruit industry particularly hard. Not all the strawberry crop, for instance, could be picked. 'The fruit is literally rotting in the fields,' said Gilbert Savory, a strawberry-grower from Herefordshire. 'We have lost £900,000 worth so far, and the season is only halfway through. It makes your heart bleed.' The result was that British growers could supply less than half the domestic market; the rest had to be imported (Michela Wrong, *Financial Times*, 15 July 2000).

Where sufficient seasonal workers were available, the results were good. The early spring-onion crop on the Norfolk House Farm was picked, cut and packed by Latvians, Lithuanians, Ukrainians, Poles, Czechs and Belarussians, recruited either directly or through gang masters. Farmers in the area were very pleased with their foreign workers – locals, they said, would not accept such work or did it badly. Elsewhere in Europe, Moroccans picked tomatoes and peppers in the hothouses of south-eastern Spain; Poles picked crops in Germany; Sikhs picked fruit in Belgium; Caribbeans picked tomatoes and fruit in Ontario and Florida (*Economist*, 6 May 2000).

Other parts of the British economy did less well. For example, Indian restaurants – now employing more workers than the British steel industry – complained of the difficulties in finding chefs, waiters and kitchen staff. The second generation of Indian immigrants, like the Chinese, too often wanted to go to university and join the professions, not run cheap restaurants and takeaways. Other sectors suffered from a lack of workers. In August 2000, the Home Secretary said he wanted to change the law to allow the British police to recruit 4,000 officers from the EU; it was, he said, impossible to keep native recruits because they could so easily get better-paid jobs elsewhere, and there were no volunteers from the other two possible sources – Ireland (where the economy was the fastest-growing in Europe) and the Commonwealth (presumably he meant the *white* Commonwealth). Similarly, there were great problems in staffing an expansion of the National Health Service; British hospitals had long recruited nurses and doctors abroad, and that seemed now the only solution. The former President of South Africa, Nelson Mandela, issued a warning against Britain poaching medical staff from South Africa, which needed all the people it had for local care.

A severe shortage of workers and tight immigration controls were the causes of a massive growth in illegal immigration.

Illegal migration

The migration of those without adequate documents was essentially a journey to work. But the tighter the immigration controls designed to prevent this, the greater the incentive to try and settle in order to make access to work more secure. The worker was forced to become a citizen, to become an exile from his or her homeland as a means to make the right to work secure. The result was paradoxical. Preventing people working so that they would not become citizens forced them to become citizens in order to work. The periodic amnesties showed that governments ultimately could not make illegality stick when the demand for labour was so great and the numbers of undocumented workers so large.

The problem was relatively new in much of Europe, deriving from the creation of the laws which defined legal migration in the 1960s and 1970s. But it was not until the 1980s and 1990s that the numbers became significant. In the US, as we have seen, Mexican migration to the north is as old as the intensive farming which requires many hands. The normal seasonal flow was made illegal by the ending of the Braceros programme in the 1960s, signalling the end of legal seasonal migration.

The new legal arrangements created not only new illegalities, but also a class of professionals devoted to defeating the law by helping people without the right papers to cross borders. The more strict and intimidating the controls, the more elaborate the means to defeat them (particularly where long-distance travel through many countries was required) and the more expensive the process became – the poorest majority often could not scrape together the means to pay the smugglers.

The guesses as to numbers are as varied as the assumptions – and prejudices – of the people who make them. The British Home Office, exercising rare statistical heroism, estimated that in 1997 there were 30 million border crossings worldwide by people without proper papers. But the existing stock of those who live somewhere they are not legally supposed to defies such guesses. The police say some 50 organisations handle this worldwide movement with degrees of specialisation – planning particular routes, destinations, forms of transport and so forth. Five groups were said to handle movement from India to Britain, ten from China to Europe.

However, while it may be fun to speculate about major international criminal syndicates, smuggling is often an industry of small businesses: hundreds of thousands of small operators, trawling for customers in the areas most migrants come from, selling them on, stage by stage, to a destination that may not be clear until the migrant arrives. Take the case of Sri Lanka, a small country savaged by a bloody and bitter civil war for nearly three decades. A journalist in Colombo in 1995 counted over 1,000 'travel agents'. Sri Lankan migrant couriers have been intercepted in the Philippines, Fiji, Turkey, the Netherlands, Albania, Austria, Zambia, Mozambique, Poland, Belarus, Lithuania (27 per cent of all 'transient migrants' detained in Lithuania in the first two thirds of 1996 were Sri Lankans), France, Slovakia, the Czech Republic, China, Pakistan, Italy and no doubt other places. Indeed, in 1997, the Tamil Refugee International Network claimed there were 20,000 Sri Lankans marooned in 12 countries of Asia, Africa and Europe – 5,000 kicking their heels in both Russia and Thailand. It was a terrible comment on the diaspora of a people driven to flee by civil war but now caught in the legal no-man's-land between the fortresses of states.

The European police, as we have noted, chose to identify illegal migration as essentially criminal activity. Yet the majority of clandestine migrants were doing jobs, most of them legal, that needed to be done but which the Europeans would not themselves do. And they did not cross borders illegally.

> Some of the thousands of Slovaks, Romanians, Poles or even Russians on whom Berliners and Londoners now rely to cut their hair, clean their houses or serve them coffee, have arrived legally on visas as students or au pairs, and stayed on illegally.

> *Economist*, 16 October 1999

Controls had made working illegal. For the workers, the obstacles put in their way in seeking work – legal, financial, physical – were just part of the natural order of things, the natural obstruction to be expected of inimical government.

Sometimes the costs were very high. Take again the example of emigrants from Fujian province in China offered jobs in a New York garment factory or restaurant kitchen (Chin, 1999). Between 1991 and 1993, 36 ships carrying 5,300 potential garment workers and dishwashers were stopped by US coastguards as they tried to enter New York (part, according to the INS, of the 100,000 Chinese illegal entrants to the US). Half of them, like those suffocated crossing the English Channel in mid-2000 started from Changle in Fujian. The average cost was US$30,000, the average journey time 106 days, though some took up to a year. The lucky ones travelled by air on stolen passports and visas. The traveller pays 10–20 per cent of the fare in advance, perhaps part of the rest along the way, and the final settlement on arrival. To ensure they are paid, the 'snakeheads' imprison the migrant, forcing relatives and friends to pay, adding torture, assault and rape to give urgency to the demands, and promise that families left behind in China will be dealt with if the migrant fails to pay. At worst, the horrors can leave the migrant maimed, permanently damaged. But astonishingly, the majority survive, and claim to pay off their debts to friends, relatives or employers within two years (with a range of between six months and four years) by working days of 12 hours, 6 days a week.

Other reports give different figures – US$15,000 from China to Britain, five years on average to meet the debts incurred – but document the same regime of violence until the smuggler is paid. However, at the other end, the effect is dramatic. The migrant's family become, by local standards, rich; able to rebuild their houses, equip themselves with household goods and cars, put children through school and university. The Changle branch of the Bank of China reports that in the mid-1990s, monthly remittance payments from migrants abroad to local families totalled some US$45 million.

Not all migration requires long-distance planning and organisation. Some migrants need help for only a part of the way – as with the 'coyotes' (Mexico's equivalent of the snakeheads) who shepherd people across the southern US border, the container truck drivers who carry them across the English Channel, or Albanian fisherman who pilot people to Italy. Others run their own smuggling routes without outside help – Dana Diminescu made a study of Roma from 11 villages in northern Romania who have regularly travelled clandestinely to Paris for seasonal work in construction and street-selling since 1992 (they sent home on average from US$3,109 to $4,664 per season per worker), for all the world as if this were still the nineteenth century and border controls did not exist.

Part of this movement – but only part – was to supply workers to the black economy, the mass of activities not officially registered. The range of activities was enormous – from small restaurants, garment shops and construction sites, to casual household workers, door-to-door and street sellers (especially of smuggled goods). Sometimes registered companies employed undocumented workers as subcontractors in unregistered subsidiaries. Sometimes the activities were not just illegal but criminal.

Conditions could be very bad. But the very worst conditions were reserved for those who fell into the hands of the slave dealers, those who traffic in women and children for prostitution and bonded labour.

Trafficking

Those who hired professionals to smuggle them across the world and into another country had to trust them without any support from the legal system. Sometimes the trust was betrayed – the agent made off with the deposit, or shipped workers to the destination without a return ticket or straight into the arms of the police. Other agents abandoned their flocks when threatened by the police: boats were sunk, with mass drowning; groups crossing the deserts of Arizona or the mountains of Switzerland died of thirst or exposure. But there were enough reliable cases to encourage many more customers to entrust themselves to the smugglers.

However, some of the more vulnerable migrants – particularly women and children – were moved on from smugglers to traffickers, from being helped to cross borders for work to being traded as slaves in prostitution, bonded labour, creatures used in pornographic films or shows, couriers for narcotic gangs or, for men, hoodlums to protect petty gangsters and narcotic dealers. Many more were simply kidnapped or seduced by the promise of work. Controls created and sustained a new segment of the global criminal world and revived the ancient trade in slaves.

The numbers involved can only be guessed. A US presidential report of the late 1990s put the world total of women and children traded for criminal purposes at 700,000, without suggesting how many exist in total. 50,000 are said to enter the US for sexual or other purposes. The evidence worldwide of where they come from and where they go is very fragmentary – occasional cases are documented, for example of mass kidnapping by racketeers in parts of China, stealing women for brothels or bonded labour in the coastal cities and Hong Kong, some of whom may end up on international circuits. The same is true of the supply of Nepalese women to Bombay's red-light zone. There are reports of auctions in Karachi to distribute women from Sri Lanka, India, Bangladesh and Pakistan to markets in the Middle East and beyond. There are other notorious flows: of Nigerian and Albanian women to Italy; of Burmese women to Thailand (returning to bring Aids to the central highlands); of Thai and Filipina women to Japan; of Russian women to Japan and East Asia, to Egypt and Western Europe; of women from Eastern Europe and the former Soviet Union to Berlin, London, Brussels, Milan and Amsterdam. Wherever there is a breakdown of order – as for example in Kosovo and Albania – kidnappers and traffickers trawl the refugee camps. But even in times of order, they are also searching villages – in say, Poland – with the offer of a job as a dancer and transport – to a destination where they are simply sold for as little as US$1,000 (£660 or so) to traders and thus on to the pimps.

Muddling the illegal international movement of ordinary workers with the trafficking in women and children makes the criminal activities disappear in the far greater flows of those moving to work, and therefore less easy for the police to target precisely. The fortification of borders stops neither illegal migrants nor slaves, so ending controls would not qualitatively change the dimensions of the problem, only make the target of police action much more accurate.

Illegal migrants for work are not just muddled with criminals. The most damaging confusion, as in the British case in Appendix I, is with those seeking sanctuary – at the cost of the right to asylum. It is almost impossible to migrate legally to Europe, North America and Japan, and so it is accordingly impossible for those in flight from terror to reach a destination where they can make a claim for refugee status – except illegally. If governments regard illegal entry as a criminal act, it invalidates any claim to asylum. In the late 1990s, the xenophobic frenzy stirred by the competition between governments and opposition in Europe was redirected from the most downtrodden group of workers, the unskilled, to an even worse off group, those fleeing their country for fear of their lives. The paradoxes of compassion seem to know no end.

Asylum-seekers

The number of refugees in the world is relatively small – around 24 million according to the UN, or not quite 0.4 per cent of the world's population. About 14 million are outside their native country. Nine hundred thousand of these (or about four in every hundred of those displaced worldwide) are in the developed countries, so the overwhelming majority of people internationally displaced, 96 per cent, are in the rest of the world. Tables 7–9 give details of the breakdown for the developed countries.

There are two principles at stake in the issue of asylum: Article 13(2) of the 1948 UN Universal Declaration of Human Rights, which proclaims the right of all to leave the country in which they live, and the 1951 Convention relating to the Status of Refugees, which states the grounds on which a person may seek asylum in another country, affirms the right of those in flight not to be returned by force to the country from which they are fleeing, and accords permission to those in flight, if necessary, to enter a country without proper documents, provided that they report to the authorities as soon as possible with a proper explanation.

As we have seen, the European governments, and to a lesser extent the US, exercised much ingenuity in trying to dodge these principles. They did this in Europe in part by disputing the evidence of persecution, and so accusing applicants of being 'bogus', illegal immigrants to be expelled, forcibly returned to the country of their nationality (even if they did not live there). In fact, as we have seen, tightening controls made it impossible to migrate legally. There was no 'refugee visa' (and no likelihood that, if one existed, consulates would issue it), so those in flight had to use a tourist, business or student visa or enter clandestinely and then claim refugee status. Yet governments took illegal entry as evidence of an intention to defraud, evidence that the asylum-seeker was bogus. As the UN (Morrison, 2000) concludes:

> If European governments were ever successful in stopping organised illegal migration at source or in transit countries, they would have ended European asylum policy as we know it.

The climate of disbelief created by governments in Europe about people claiming asylum had its effect. Immigration officials treated cases with a carelessness and an impatience remarkable in a public policy supposedly devoted to showing compassion. As the British Minister of State, with supreme confidence, put it in a Commons debate (9 November 1999): 'People come here with *manifestly unfounded* [italics added] claims'. Press and politicians reiterated the litany that the refugees were fraudulent to the point where it became common-sense – and a matter of ridicule to take seriously the tales of hideous persecution. It was one thing to be horrified by a television presentation of the agony of Sarajevo or Rwanda, quite another to extend that concern when the issue was presented on the doorstep. Compassion, it seemed, was strictly for the people who stayed somewhere else.

It would have been surprising if some political leaders or government officials were not embarrassed by this display of both duplicity and callousness. In confidence, perhaps they discussed getting rid of the wretched right of asylum in order to relieve the hypocrisy. After all, the EU Protocol Treaty of Amsterdam (November 1997) removed – or at least curtailed – the right of Europeans to claim asylum in another EU country, and without much protest. Presumably that meant that Europeans could be deported by force back to their home country? During the Austrian presidency of the EU in 1998, a draft strategy document suggested ending the right to asylum, leaving it to the discretion of governments (and bilateral agreements between governments) as to whether to grant refugee status. The governments did not proceed, presumably fearing protests.

A sub-theme in the debate is political. The right of asylum is always political in that it is related not so much to the persecution of individuals, however horrific that might be, but to the countries from which they are fleeing. In the days of the Cold War, for the US refugees meant people fleeing from the Soviet Union or its allies, or from China and Cuba. There were, by definition, no refugees fleeing from Chile, Argentina or Brazil as the result of military coups and severe repression. Without that sure star to guide the way, criteria become foggy. Countries which are clearly experiencing major catastrophes of civil war or collapse might earn favourable treatment for their citizens claiming to be refugees. But for most countries this does not work. A terrified arrival from Sudan, for example, can be recommended – with a straight face – to return there and apply for protection to the local courts. Turkey is a difficult country. The evidence of torture is notorious, but Turkey is a friend, a member of NATO, a potential member of the EU. The claims of those in flight from Turkey, mainly Kurds, are treated with suspicion. It is almost impossible for someone from India to get refugee status in Britain. The torments of individuals are remote from the issues of government-to-government relations.

What is the evidence, so obvious to ministers, that most asylum-seekers are bogus? Only an independent and open tribunal, devoted to protecting the right of asylum, can be expected to produce some consistency here. But it is naïve to expect governments to allow the reduction in their room to manoeuvre which would follow relinquishing control of their borders to an independent body. Short of this, the evidence is circumstantial. The bulk of applications (see Tables 7 and 8) are from people coming from countries which are indeed recognised as being in a severe state of breakdown: Iraq, Afghanistan, Somalia, former Yugoslavia, Algeria, Colombia. The rest are from countries with major civil disorders, civil wars or notorious records in the abuse of human rights (for example Sri Lanka and Turkey). But evidence, such as bullet-holes in backs or the burns across the chests, interests no one primarily concerned with ending immigration.

The policy outcome of these difficulties is to try to make conditions even worse to deter people from coming. An increasing number of those arriving are now imprisoned, either in special detention camps or, contrary to the UN ruling, in ordinary prisons – without trial or appeal and for indefinite periods. In the British case, some 15 per cent of applicants (or about 10,000 per year) are currently detained, or 700–1,000 at any one time. In 2000, the government announced a major expansion in detention centres by the year 2001. The leader of the opposition went one step further, to prove he could be more vicious in his compassion than the government, and promised that all asylum-seekers would be detained if he came to power – and presumably the families broken up, children taken into care.

For those not detained (imprisoned in real terms), conditions are to be increasingly draconian. Under the British Asylum and Immigration Act (2000), the financial allowance for asylum-seekers was cut to 75 per cent of what was considered adequate for subsistence at that time: £36.40 per week for an individual, payable in vouchers tied to 'necessities', with a £10 cash allowance for other expenses. This is paid only if the applicant agrees to be 'dispersed', sent to housing in an out-of-London location and with other conditions. If asylum-seekers receive material help from other sources, NGOs or charities, this is to be deducted from the allowance.

Such a regime is so dreadful it can have little appeal to economic migrants, whose aim is to work and earn, not wait for six months – indefinitely in Germany. Those who can withstand this regime – a sort of medieval torture test to separate true and false – can be presumed to be genuine refugees. But it is difficult, on any rational basis, to see why they should be treated so shockingly. In practice, many applicants just disappear – giving up the supposedly lavish benefits from the public purse – rather than be separated from friends and relatives. Once disappeared, they can become ordinary illegal migrants, able to look for work and thus much better off than when trapped in the misery of asylum-seeking.

Did asylum-seekers 'shop around' for the best deal on offer, for the 'soft touch'? Indeed, as they fled in fear of their lives, did they have any idea of the complicated regulations and rights put in place by various governments? The Spanish government explained what was said to be a sudden increase in illegal immigration in August 2000 as migrants responding to proposed new legislation in September which would make arrest and expulsion quicker. But was it true – or even plausible? The then-British Home Secretary,

Jack Straw, told the House of Commons (9 November 1999) that if
the system of cash payments (instead of the proposed vouchers)
were kept, asylum applications would increase by 40,000, and that
'there is no doubt that the costs would run to £400 or £500 million'.
The conscientious recorders of the speech did not report whether
he blushed at this heroic invention. He cited no evidence, and it is
difficult to know what evidence there could be for such a figure.
But he and his department hardly cared or needed to care for such
details – they had the tide of opinion with them.

There is some evidence. A 1998 EU survey showed that asylum-
seekers head for places where there are relatives or people they
know, or where the smugglers want to take them. 'In the majority
of cases, the choice of country for asylum is not a conscious, rational
choice by the asylum-seeker, and certainly not based on a comparison
of the advantages and disadvantages of various options.' This is not
a very astonishing conclusion, except in the hothouse atmosphere
of parliament, dominated by a sense of paranoia, where fine tooling
of the regulations is about all the MPs can do.

There is still more to be done to stop the flow. To speed up
processing (or the process of refusing applications), the British
immigration authorities considered concentrating it at the point of
arrival – while the person, with no doubt deficient English, no
knowledge of what was required and no interpreter or legal adviser
in attendance, was still exhausted from the escape and the journey.
A secret pilot scheme was launched at Heathrow to make instant
decisions, allowing five days for an appeal to be lodged.

Conclusions

It is a shameful sorry story, one of injustice, myopia and bad faith.
The hypocrisy which governs the debate is only slightly better than
the enraged and self-righteous inventions of the press. And what
possible justification is there? Even if some of the asylum-seekers
are bogus, whatever that could mean, the numbers are so small it is
absurd that it should provide the focus for a national obsession.

The Europeans, and to a lesser extent the Americans, have built a
set of legal and physical fortifications which make legal immigration –

outside a few selected groups – virtually impossible. Given the grave labour shortage, illegal immigration inevitably expands, but given the growing restrictions, it becomes increasingly expensive and hazardous. And it requires the talents of those professionally devoted to defeating governments. The measures – blanket enforcement, common visa policies and readmission treaties in Europe, carrier sanctions, measures to prevent leaving home and arrival in Europe, detention, forced repatriation, employer sanctions, random police and workplace checks – add up to a regime of terrorism, directed most often on racial grounds. Under what is supposed to be a rule of law, it is lawless.

The underlying principle of the approach is that the world of migration is only for the professional and highly skilled, a privilege for the elite (Appendix IV shows how Singapore made this distinction explicit). Those counted as unskilled are to be tied, like serfs, to the soil of their homeland and denied the opportunity to work. This is the new world of capitalist freedoms.

3 — Why Control Immigration? Reactions and Arguments

The newcomers

The arrival of lots of newcomers in a country, looking strange, eating strange food and dressing in strange ways, speaking unknown tongues, can frighten the people who live there. But it is by no means inevitable. In fact, despite the popular view – as displayed in much of the press and among politicians – that violent reaction is unavoidable, such responses are relatively rare. If we were to add up the cases of serious conflict, involving many people, they would be small compared to the much more frequent quiet acceptance by the mass of the population. Consider the three million Afghans who were temporarily absorbed in Pakistan, or roughly the same number taken into Iran. Irritations, quarrels, clashes and discrimination no doubt occurred, but not on the scale approaching the fantasies of race war that inflame some fevered imaginations. Nothing in Europe and North America compares to this scale of movement of people. Indeed, is xenophobic conflict as great as that from other kinds of clashes – from riots over rising prices to strikes over pay and layoffs and demonstrations?

In the developed countries, you might say, matters are different. The mild xenophobia that seems to affect most people most of the time but sometimes affects a minority in more rabid forms rarely turns into mass violence, certainly more rarely than other forms of violence (at football matches, for example). But the position of the state makes matters different. The government taxes heavily, dominates the economy, and distributes certain benefits to the population. Who shares in this system – paying and receiving – adds a different dimension to simply reacting to newcomers. They are supposedly new claims on the share-out – and something for them, people reason, means less for everyone else. This can become a more pressing issue when people feel economically deprived – then the share-out is seen as being at their expense and they consequently believe newcomers should not 'be allowed to lay claim to what ought to be the exclusive privilege of the native.

Yet even then any real movement of opposition to immigration requires political leadership. It is here that the problems begin. Politicians who play the 'race card' often claim only to be expressing what the majority of people feel. They are doing their job in giving a public airing to fears and resentments – even if they privately deplore the opinions they express. But if innocent, that is naïve. They are shaping perceptions, leading them, in some cases creating them – as a means of coming to power or staying in power.

Even when the number of immigrants are tiny, a politician can turn them into a disaster. Consider an Australian case in Autumn 1999. A dilapidated freighter from Indonesia was intercepted off the northern coast of Australia. A total of 70 boats had landed illegally over the preceding three months, with mainly Chinese passengers, but also, towards the end, Afghans and Iraqis. In two weeks there had been a total of seven boats carrying 450 passengers in total.

The *Financial Times* (19 October 1999) reported Philip Ruddock, Australia's Minister of Immigration, as saying that 'It was a national emergency several weeks ago. It's gone up something like 10 points on the Richter scale since then', and that the 'onslaught' was part of possibly '10,000 people about to set sail', according to an 'intelligence report'. Sadly Ruddock is not known to have been reproved by his government for being just plain silly.

It is not at all inevitable that political leaders need to do this. Hugh Gaitskell, leader of the Labour opposition to the First Commonwealth Immigration Bill in Britain in 1962 presented a clear rejection of controls. In a speech to demonstrators in Trafalgar Square, he asked, 'What is the reason for this Bill? The immigrants are healthy, law-abiding and are at work. They are helping us. Why, then, do the government wish to keep them out? It is because they are coloured.' He was right. William Deedes, Conservative minister without portfolio, admitted that the 1962 Commonwealth Immigration Act's 'real purpose was to restrict the influx of coloured immigrants' but 'we were reluctant to say as much openly'. Gaitskell later said in the House of Commons, 'It is in my opinion an utter and complete myth that there is the slightest danger of millions and millions of brown and black people coming to this country. Anyone who is trying to put that across is only trying to frighten people into believing it.' However, by 1964 Labour had reversed its position, as was made clear by former minister Richard Crossman: 'Ever since the Smethwick election, it has been quite clear that immigration can be the greatest potential vote loser for the Labour Party if we are seen as permitting a flood of immigrants to come in and blight the central areas of our cities'.

The political centre has usually been much more ambiguous, sometimes flirting with racism, sometimes opposing it – and it is there that the trouble lies. They are ambiguous, they say, because they are afraid of xenophobia, of the nightmare of race war. But in compromising with xenophobia, they encourage it, lead it. It is not accidental that when politicians choose to make an issue of new arrivals – as, for example, in the case of asylum-seekers in recent years – racist attacks increase sharply.

This is not the work of the overtly anti-immigration parties – Haider's Freedom Party in Austria, the Democratic Union of the Centre in Switzerland, Vlaams Block in Belgium or the National Front in France (and earlier in Britain) – which have failed to build an alternative of substance on the basis of what a Flemish newspaper calls the politics of 'fear, intolerance, plain racism and law and order'. It is rather the political centre or conservative right wing. The examples already given are by no means the only ones. France's former president Giscard d'Estaing once spoke of the 'foreign invasion' of France; one-time Prime Minister Edith Cresson promised the mass expulsion of illegal immigrants. Charles Pasqua, as minister in 1993, proposed a target of 'zero immigration', promising to legislate for random police identity checks and accel- erated expulsions because illegal immigrants were 'responsible for crime and drug dealing'. In the regional elections of April 2000, the leader of the right-wing opposition in Italy, Silvio Berlusconi, campaigned on an anti-immigrant platform.

Consider a German example. The Social Democratic Chancellor, Gerhard Schroeder, proposed to make it easier for those not of German descent to get German nationality by revising the 1913 Citizenship Code. It was a modest proposal, modifying a clear long-standing injustice – that the descendants of immigrants could never stop being 'immigrants', even if their ancestors had lived in Germany for several generations. But still the Christian Democrats put up a stout opposition – until they learned that sections of German business favoured the reform. In the year 2000, the Chancellor raised the issue that Germany had too few highly skilled IT professionals, and proposed they be brought in from India and Eastern Europe – 20,000 on five-year visas. Christian Democrat leader Jurgen Ruttgers fought the May state elections for North Rhine – Westphalia on the slogan 'Kinder Staat Inder' – 'educate German children, not import Indians' – as if this was a serious alternative. He lost. But another Christian Democrat promised to campaign on the issue of opposition to immigration in the 2002 elections; hopefully those who care about the economic future of Germany will be able to sideline him.

It is not that these arguments are unpleasant. They are often fraudulent, lies – and lies which go unchallenged. The presence or absence of foreigners is irrelevant to the problems facing people. Politicians compete, as was recently seen on the asylum issue, to be 'tough', which means allowing xenophobia or racism its head in the name of realism. It is fortunate, given the centre's flirtation with danger and the predisposition to xenophobia among people at large, that there has not been more success in creating a serious movement to repel foreigners.

However, there is, for many people, a strange predisposition to blaming foreigners for whatever goes wrong. It is made worse when immigrants fill the lowest-paid jobs. Then the ferocious and unforgiving popular contempt for the poor and the lowliest labourer comes into play, linked to fantasy hates: the dirty, the undisciplined, the lazy, the sponger, the parasite, all compound the xenophobia.

The reaction is made worse by the mythological character of the 'Third World', as presented in press and television – a world of famine and social chaos, of beggars, rampant corruption and vicious dictators. It is a picture which excludes most of the reality.

It is as if North America or Europe were to be defined by one terrible disaster, a hurricane or flood or mass killing. However, the fears about being overwhelmed by this nightmare of countless millions remain.

> We are faced with the fact that some large percentage – and it could be a very large percentage – of the earth's four billion non-US inhabitants would opt, if they could, to leave where they are now and come to this country. If that happened, Lifeboat America would quickly sink.

> Rodger Lewis, *Wall Street Journal*, 30 November 1981

Consider the UK, a country with a long tradition of anti-immigration politicians. As early as 1902, in a speech in the House of Commons on 29 January, British MP Evan Gordon demanded immigration controls and railed against the 'foreign invaders' whom he claimed were displacing native Britons:

> Not a day passes but English families are ruthlessly turned out to make room for…Romanians, Russians and Poles. Rents are raised 50 or 100 per cent…It is only a matter of time before the population becomes entirely foreign…The working classes know that the new buildings are erected not for them but for strangers from abroad; they see schools crowded with foreign children, and the very posters and advertisements on the wall in a foreign tongue.

By the 1960s, European 'invaders' had become acceptable; the target was now black people. During the by-election campaign at Smethwick in Britain in 1964 the Conservative Party candidate condoned the slogan, 'If you want a nigger for a neighbour, vote Labour', widely used by local children. Instead of condemning his opponent's racism, Labour's candidate, former cabinet minister Patrick Gordon Walker, replied feebly, 'Be fair. Immigrants only arrived in Smethwick in large numbers during the past ten years – while the Tory government was in power. You can't blame Labour or Gordon Walker for that.'

Tory MP Enoch Powell's infamous anti-immigrant speech of 20 April 1968 – 'As I look ahead, I am filled with foreboding. Like the Roman, I see "the River Tiber foaming with much blood"' – was widely and roundly condemned for its racism, but both then and later his views were echoed, albeit in much less extreme terms, by other right-wing politicians. In January 1978, Margaret Thatcher, then leader of the Conservative Party, declared,

I do not believe it is in human nature that…a country such as ours should passively watch the transformation of whole areas which lie in the heart of it into alien territory…by the end of the century there would be four million people of the New [i.e. black] Commonwealth or Pakistan here. Now that is an awful lot, and I think it means that people are really rather afraid that this country might be rather swamped by people of a different culture…If there is a fear of being swamped people are going to be rather hostile to those coming in.

Lord Norman Tebbit complained that 'great waves of immigration by people who do not share our culture, our language, our way of social conduct, in many cases who owe no allegiance to our country,' were 'a destabilising factor in society'. Such nonsense helps to create public fear and resentment of immigration universally, and focussed on immigrants' main entry points – for example El Paso in Texas, Dover in southern England, the Spanish enclaves of Ceuta and Melilla in Morocco, the Apulian coast or Polish–German frontier – as beleaguered bastions manned by heroic defenders of the state. The crowds loved it, the governments took full advantage of what was an easy target. The drama justified tough action (public attention might otherwise have been deflected towards a compassion for the vulnerability of those seeking work), so harsher controls were introduced and more 'heroic defenders' deployed.

In this situation, only the immigration officer stands between this mythic small corner of civilisation and the fantasy of a vast encroaching jungle of barbarism.

The gap between fears and reality is made worse by the daily deluge of misinformation which encourages and seems to confirm these terrors. As we saw in the case of Australia, a trivial incident can be exploited to turn fears into panic, 'the end of civilisation as we know it'. Fear and political leadership go some way towards explaining the startling range of false opinion that so many people have about immigration. For example, the *New York Times* (14 July 1986) commissioned a survey which showed that virtually half of the population believed most recent immigrants to the US were illegal, and that this was a severe economic problem. Other polls show equally large numbers believing that illegal immigrants impose heavy costs on government and taxpayers. The evidence, easily available, is, as we shall see later, the opposite. The 'problem' is not with illegal immigrants but with people's perceptions of illegal immigrants.

It is not just mass opinion which is in the grip of fantasy. Consider a major scientific study, *The New Americans* (National Research Council, 1997), on the face of it a well balanced and judicial summing up of the wealth of research on immigration in the US. At various stages, the authors make observations such as: 'As long as there is a virtually unlimited supply of potential immigrants, the nation has to make choices about how many immigrants to admit'; or: 'Although not everyone outside the United States wishes to or realistically will seek to emigrate to the United States'; or again: 'Immigration to the United States should be attractive to most workers from less economically developed countries and…Skilled workers from many developed countries may want to emigrate to the United States'.

Is it vanity – a belief that life in the US is so beautiful that no one can resist it – or fear that allows such preposterous statements? The numbers of people moving to the US (allowing also for emigration from the US), legally and illegally, is tiny compared both to the population of the world and that of the US. Without immigration controls, is there evidence that, even if it increased, it would still be anything other than tiny? If Florida, say, is attractive, why does not everybody in the US move there? Most people in the world do not move, and do not want to move, and as we shall see, it is certainly not the poor who move, nor is it controls that prevent them.

The fears dominate the newspaper headlines, so the opposite trends get precious little publicity. Governments are aware of the dangers of an outbreak of compassion for the victims rather than rage against the invaders. Appendix III shows the British Hong Kong administration choosing three o'clock in the morning, while the world slept, to deport forcibly the first batch of Vietnamese boatpeople, lest the press incite protests at this inhumanity.

Often the press barely covers the counter-evidence. For example, citizen outrage at random police checks of passers-by on the street (selected by colour of skin) or worker anger at government invasions of workplaces or factories or farms, a rage which in the US is transmitted through local congressmen and constrains the official arms of government.

Take the case of Lexington, Nebraska reported in the *Economist* (16 October 1999). The old city economy, based on making tractors, collapsed in the 1970s and jobs disappeared – everyone was selling up and leaving, until a giant meat-packing plant moved in and revived the whole place. It employed mainly Latinos, with a few Asians – on wages for dangerous and dirty jobs that was well below what used to be paid 20 years earlier. But the city boomed once again. Then the INS sniffed out possibly illegal immigrants.

The INS used to make armed raids on factories to check on the night shift, but it caused a lot of understandable outrage. So it introduced Operation Vanguard to check work documents regularly. Out of 24,000 worker records, 4,441 discrepancies were found in the plant. Before the INS was able to interview them, three quarters disappeared, which meant they lost their jobs, which is what the INS wanted.

The INS was happy, but not the employers. They were furious at the disruption and at having to search for so many more new recruits in an area with a great shortage of such workers. They complained bitterly to their elected representatives, who in turn upbraided the INS, demanding more leniency for illegal immigrants. Employers started donating to Latino causes to protect illegals. As Ben Nelson, ex-governor of the state, put it, 'I don't expect the INS to run the agency based on what's best for Nebraska agriculture, but I don't expect them to go out of their way to come up with a programme that kicks agriculture right in the shins'.

Trade unions have become important in protecting immigrants. Traditionally unions have opposed immigration as bringing in competitors for the jobs of their members. But the long scorching period of decline in membership has shifted many of them to see immigrants, legal or illegal, as potential members. The American Federation of Labour – Congress of Industrial Relations (AFL–CIO) in the US has been a major force pressing for amnesties for illegal immigrants and an end to penalties on employers for hiring illegal immigrants. In Britain, the Trades Union Congress (TUC) and some of its member organisations have been important in the campaign against, for example, the government's asylum policy. Churches and other religious bodies have also often been important. In the mid-1980s, American churches, synagogues and religious meeting houses, 281 of them, organised a clandestine system to smuggle refugees to sanctuaries in the US – to the fury of the INS and the government, which in October 1985 endeavoured to lay criminal charges against the offenders. San Francisco bravely declared itself 'city of refuge for gay illegals'. The head of the German Catholic Church, in the same spirit, in 1994 called on local priests to offer sanctuary for refugees facing deportation, and there were other important campaigns – by Danes against the long-term imprisonment of Palestinian refugees; by British campaigners against the Asylum Bill and refugee imprisonment in Campsfield and other detention centres; by the Belgian and French '*sans papiers*' movement (proclaiming 'No freedom of movement for capital without freedom of movement for people'); and by German activists, adopting the slogan 'No one is illegal', seeking to hide and support illegal migrants, to help people across borders and oppose deportations. In Switzerland, with the second-highest number of foreign-born people in Europe, six national referenda have thrown out the proposal to limit immigrants to a particular share of the population; in the last vote, in September 2000, 64 per cent of the voters rejected a proposal to limit foreigners to 18 per cent of the population (they were then 19.3 per cent). But somehow all this seemed flimsy stuff to many journalists alongside one minor punch-up between natives and foreigners.

The press was not universally xenophobic, but the opposition tended to come only from businesspeople. The *Wall Street Journal* was notorious for supporting free immigration. Others attacked the desperately cruel treatment of refugees. In London, the *Financial Times* regularly deplored the racism of successive British governments in relation to immigration. For example, for a time before China took back Hong Kong in 1997, the British parliament debated endlessly who in the city should be offered British passports. In August 1989, the *Financial Times* economics editor, Samuel Brittain, noted that if Britain accepted the whole of Hong Kong's population the numbers would be small – if entries were staggered over the remaining eight years until the 1997 accession, the annual increase would be about 0.7 per cent of the British population (or close to the ordinary rate of increase). Hong Kong workers were skilled in some of the activities most scarce in Britain, younger than the average British worker and with higher levels of education. If they could be persuaded to come, they would expand the whole British economy, and increase the number of jobs available for the British and also government tax revenues. They could revive whole areas in the poorer north. Why did the government not rush to capture such a desirable workforce? 'It would be kinder not to speculate, but the reasons can have little to do with Britain's economic performance.' Or, we might add the welfare of the British. In the same newspaper, Philip Stephens (23 June 2000) noted that, after the 58 Chinese illegal immigrants had been found suffocated to death in a container truck at Dover, the Portugal meeting of the 15 EU leaders expressed no more than nominal regret; they were mainly enraged at the smugglers who made money out of the victims, and the need to tighten controls.

Mild or extreme xenophobia was the more common norm. This was particularly true when politically important figures publicly championed such views. At the other extreme, as Rita Simons (1985,1993) notes, are American economists (including 38 former Presidents of the American Economic Association). Eighty-one per cent regarded immigration as being very favourable for economic growth and the other 19 per cent thought it slightly favourable. Fifty-six per cent wanted more immigration, 33 per cent the continuing of existing levels, the rest were unsure. It settles nothing – economists have no claim to infallibility. And despite their opinions, their voices counted for little. But the divergence of views does raise questions about the astonishing gap in perceptions.

People's fears are real enough: fears of radical change which will destroy their way of life or make it very much worse, make their qualifications worthless, force them into poverty. But immigration is hardly ever relevant to these processes of wrenching economic change. The rapid decline of farming as a way of life or the devastation in the 1970s of the heavy and engineering industries of the Ruhr, of Gary–Indiana, of Pittsburgh or Detroit, or the West Midlands and Birmingham have nothing to do with immigrants. Perhaps those who have lost their livelihoods do not care what the explanation is, but want only to express their anger and inflict it not upon unreal economic forces but upon some real person. They look for scapegoats.

Immigrants are an easy target. In Japan in 1999 an Economic Planning Agency survey found that 80 per cent of the population opposed increases in immigration. In the US, in almost every survey from the 1930s to 1993 a majority opposed more immigration, though a 1977 Gallup poll showed a more qualified response: 7 per cent wanted an increase, 37 per cent did not know. According to Simon (1993), the standard opinion was, 'The people who came here in earlier times were good folks, but the people who are coming now are purely scum'.

Racism is still widely considered socially acceptable. In Europe, a European Community survey of late 1997 found that 33 per cent of the sample were 'quite racist' or 'very racist'. Belgium headed the table with 22 per cent saying they were 'very racist', followed by France and Austria. Luxembourg (with the highest foreign-born population share in Europe) and Sweden had the fewest citizens who were 'very racist': 86 per cent opposed all discrimination by race, religion or culture. Other European surveys in the 1990s showed worse results. In Germany in 1998, 51 per cent said there were too many foreigners in the country. In 1996, 30 per cent of Spaniards agreed they were racist, as did nearly half of those interviewed in France, while in Belgium in 1997 the proportion was over half.

In Britain, before Margaret Thatcher's 1978 speech sympathising with those who felt 'rather swamped' by black immigrants, 9 per cent of a national poll agreed that immigration was one of the country's two most urgent problems (and support for the two main political parties was about equal at 44 per cent). After the speech, 21 per cent thought immigration one of the two main issues (and the Conservatives overtook Labour with 48 per cent to 39 per cent of the vote). Andrew Lansley, former head of research at Conservative Central Office, later said, 'Immigration, an issue we raised successfully in 1992 and again in the European election campaign, played particularly well in the tabloids and has more potential to hurt' (*Observer*, 3 September 1995).

Hating foreigners in general (as opposed to hating the particular foreigners you know) cannot easily be argued with. The disquiet felt at immigration is therefore not easily countered by evidence or logic. The rage at the treasonable betrayal of the nation is sporadic, impulsive, violent, and brings political leaders who champion this cause often massive – if temporary – popular adoration. But, fortunately, it is very rarely capable of being turned into a ladder to power. For that, a general social collapse is required.

If there can be no argument with the rage, the disquiet is more accessible. What follows is an attempt to put together some of the evidence on the issues, to show the abyss between opinion on this subject and reality.

The arguments

Immigration control reduces racism and xenophobia

The favourite argument by political leaders is that control of entries to the country, especially in the case of black workers, is the precondition for reducing racism and xenophobia. It is a most unkind argument since it blames the victims for their condition, not those who victimise them. It repeats the old antisemitic argument of the Nazis – antisemitism existed in Germany only because Jews lived there; removal of the Jews would thus end antisemitism. The methodology is impeccable – rape exists only because there are women, so removing all women would end rape.

It is, of course, pure nonsense. As we note elsewhere, racism is strongest where there are fewest black workers, and xenophobia most ferocious where there are the fewest foreigners. Thus attacks on foreigners are at their most extreme in eastern Germany where there are fewest (compared to western Germany where there are most foreigners). To follow the proper logic, the way to conquer racism in eastern Germany would be to increase the number of black workers there, and to end xenophobia to allow in more foreigners.

The case is worse than this. The national debate over immigration, over limiting entries, has played a fundamental role in increasing racism and xenophobia. Most recently, the political argument over the admission of asylum-seekers has been the most important cause of an increase in racist attacks and assaults in Europe. Appendix I shows an example of this from Britain. Far from immigration controls reassuring populations, they lead to disbelief in the effectiveness of controls (and hysteria over illegal immigration), legitimise racism under the guise of stopping immigration, and intensify discrimination against foreigners in general.

The invasion of the poor

As we have seen, a common source of panic about immigration is the idea of a world divided between a rich ordered minority in the US, Europe and Japan, and the vast majority of the desperately poor. Surely, it is suggested, given any chance, the poor will try to escape their nightmare and flee to the developed world. Immigration controls are no more than sensible defences against the regrettable failure of other countries to produce wealth. The argument hints that the issue is about theft – the poor majority want to steal from the rich minority. Elementary self-protection is needed to stop the thieves breaking in.

Governments in developed countries which use this argument – as we have seen – need to suggest that refugees are fleeing not political terror, which is allowed, but poverty, which is not. The British and Hong Kong governments turned the middle-class refugees of Vietnam, the boatpeople, into the poor to justify deporting them (see Appendix III).

Is the world divided in this way, between poverty and abundance? The idea of the Third World was originally created in the 1950s to mobilise the newly independent governments of the European ex-colonial empires to combine their bargaining power relative to the governments of the great powers. It served this aim well. But it is very far from reality – as the poor in the developed countries show. The majority is immensely mixed – from the prosperity of Singapore or South Korea, the industrial powerhouses of Bombay or Shanghai, the developed European character of Argentina, the beaches of Copacabana or Acapulco, to the desert austerity of Mali, the hideous poverty of parts of India and China, the civil wars of the horn of Africa or Angola. In fact, this *is* the world, rather than the small and declining population of the developed countries. Given the variation, it is impossible to say who would want to migrate where, but much the largest movements are within this group rather than to the developed world.

In any case, is it poverty that leads people to migrate? There are cases of catastrophe – famine, flood, war – which lead people to flee. It is this image which the press presents as the source of migration. But this is not generally the case for those who migrate to Europe and North America. They are not the poor – the sheer costs of international migration rule that out. The poorest countries do not produce emigrants, and of those countries which do it is not the poor people there who migrate. Take, for example, India. Jullundur in the Punjab has produced a large number of emigrants, yet it is one of the richer districts of a relatively rich province. The people who leave are the better-educated with family incomes that are around or above the average, not people from India's vast number of poor, who are concentrated in other provinces – eastern Uttar Pradesh, Bihar and Orissa. Of course, when they arrive at the other end, in a developed country, they join the ranks of the lower-skilled and the low-paid (even when, as in some cases, they have university degrees), but at a much higher income level than they were when they set out.

Poverty does not drive people out. To migrate internationally you need access to money well beyond the means of the poor, and some saleable qualifications. If people moved simply because of poverty, millions might indeed be on the move, whereas, as we have seen, the proportion of the population which migrates is very small. Most people – like people in developed countries – not only do not want to move, they actively resist going into exile. The nightmare of mass invasion is pure fantasy, designed to spread panic not understanding. It is the child of xenophobia.

If it is not poverty which provokes people to move, what is it? For refugees, it is a threat to life and liberty so great it makes the immense dangers and costs of flight acceptable. For economic migrants, it is the search for work and a better income than can be obtained at home. Again, the costs and risks are high, so the chance of work has to be reasonably realistic. There is too much to lose to leap into the darkness, hoping there is somewhere to land. So people move who fit the kind of jobs on offer – in age, skills and gender – and who have learned from friends and relatives, trustworthy sources, that there are indeed jobs to be had. But this is the result of opportunities in the developed countries, not of problems of the poor country. It is the failure of the developed country to meet the demand for workers that leads a small minority, possessing the education and with access to the money, to risk the adventure of migrating.

More than this, the migration of workers shows us where workers are needed, what skills are required – where (what cities or regions, and local areas within these) and when (for example, in what season). It is obvious that the need for workers of one type may coincide with high levels of unemployment for workers of a different type. Often it is not at all possible to swap one type for another (or at least the workers won't do it) – late middle-aged miners in villages in one region cannot and will not opt to replace teenage secretaries in big cities. Young Americans will not volunteer to be dishwashers in Chinese restaurants nor work in New York's notorious garment factories.

So illegal migration is not a thieving expedition to steal the jobs of the natives, nor is it feckless and irresponsible tourism. It is a straightforward rational response to the opportunity to work – and at wages that may be far too low to attract any native workers, but are far in advance of what the immigrant could earn at home (even in jobs of higher skill or education). Additionally the work often needs to be done if the natives are to get and keep better paid jobs.

The way to stop immigration is to kill the creation of jobs, to organise a slump, mass unemployment. This will be more effective than any number of controls or investing in the areas from which the immigrants come. The Great Depression of the inter-war years is a classic example – it was not the controls on entry which cut immigration to the US; it was that people were not trying to enter as they knew full well there were no jobs. A famous study of Caribbean migration to Britain in the 1950s (Jones and Smith, 1970) confirmed this – a sharp increase in unemployment in Britain turned off the tap of people moving there, but an increase in the number of jobs on offer in the Caribbean had no effect on people emigrating. But of course the governments of Europe and North America risk their political necks if they propose the organisation of mass unemployment in order to stop immigration.

The case on migration has parallels with the argument about the trade in drugs. Washington has spent an enormous sum of money, time and energy, in trying to eliminate the production of coca and the poppy in South America, South-east and South Asia in the belief that the supply can be stopped, thereby deterring Americans from using the narcotics made. But all the efforts have been a failure. Indeed, the street price of drugs in the US has not been at all affected by the attempts to destroy the production and movement of narcotics. Furthermore, in trying to do this, Washington has built and sustained a growing criminal network which is eating away at the vitals of the administration of many countries, corrupting officials and raising levels of violence in all the drug-producing countries. But while Americans continue to consume cocaine and heroin, suppliers will find a way of supplying it.

Migrants are not narcotics. Their work is needed. Despite all the obstacles – some of them terrifying – put in their way, they persist in going to work, in helping to raise the quality of life and the GDPs of the developed countries. Only mass unemployment and a severe economic slump would stop this migration – and would stop it without any need for immigration controls at all.

Do they steal jobs and depress wages for the lowest-paid?

One of the most powerful arguments for controlling immigration is that without controls immigrants will accept lower wages than the natives and either drive them out of work altogether or force them to accept pay cuts to keep their jobs. The case especially affects the worse-off workers – in the US, for example, black and Hispanic workers. The argument is even stronger with illegal immigrants, who are supposedly unable to protest against bad wages and conditions because they might be arrested and deported. Consider this commentator on American conditions (Portes, 1974):

> The native poor – those in marginal menial services and unskilled occupations...compete directly with illegal labour. Since wetbacks (Mexican illegal immigrants) are willing to work more hours for lower pay and no fringe benefits, the native worker finds himself at a disadvantage and is often completely displaced from his job. Only the poor pay the costs of illegal immigration; the sectors most severely affected by the wetback flow are precisely the ones least able to wield effective political power in defence of their interests.

Can this be true?

Most immigrants, legal and illegal, are, as we noted earlier, bunched at the two opposite ends of the skills range – the highly skilled or professional (medical doctors, engineers, software programmers, airline pilots, university teachers) and the 'unskilled' or semi-skilled (the word 'skill' is very primitive and does no justice to the complexity of the different grounds on which people are hired). They are a highly selected group – they select themselves – and heavily concentrated in the age groups with most intense work capacity. The disabled, the blind, the psychiatrically ill-equipped, single mothers, and usually the illiterate are very under-represented (compared to the 'balanced' native population) because they could not normally undertake the risks of migrating. So they are very different from an average sample of the native population in which there are none of these exclusions.

The highly skilled compete directly with the native highly skilled, though usually there are many controls (as with doctors) to make sure that the natives get the best jobs and stay on top; but here workers are competing. The immigrant professionals take the worst jobs. However, at the unskilled end, where the mass of migrants are, there is very little competition with the natives. As we suggested earlier, decades of education have lifted native workers out of this group, and once educated, their expectations do not allow them to do lowly jobs: they won't work at such pay rates or in such conditions. The conventional measure for the lowest layer of workers in the US is workers who fail to reach a high-school diploma, 'high-school drop-outs'. These accounted for about 40 per cent of American workers in 1970, but now, with steadily intensifying education, for under 10 per cent. Furthermore, many of these workers are earlier immigrants rather than natives proper. By contrast, 36 per cent of immigrants to the US in the 1990s were classed as 'high-school drop-outs' (most of them entering the US as relatives of American citizens). In sum, there is very little competition from native workers for the jobs high-school drop-outs do. Even if the effect of immigration was to lower wages and drive existing workers out of work, it would affect very few native workers – the educational system has removed them from those jobs.

Many studies in the US have tried to measure the impact of immigration on employment and pay, particularly of the worst-off workers – notoriously black ones. But it seems the black population is rarely concentrated in the small number of places where immigrants go, and often, where they do coexist, they work in different sectors. In one locality where they did coincide, a study estimated that a 10 per cent increase in immigrant workers could lead to a 0.6 per cent decline in wages for competing black workers.

However, even this cannot be assumed to be the whole truth. Immigrants expand the whole economy. They are not only workers but consumers – of housing and furnishing, food, entertainment, transport and so on, much of which is provided by the native population. This impact is very much larger than any effect on competing workers.

Furthermore, the jobs done by immigrants are 'complementary' – that is, they are required to make possible the employment of natives. As Stahl (1989) puts it: 'Insofar as skilled and unskilled are complementary factors, a shortage of one will reduce the productivity of the other'.

A study of the garment industry in Los Angeles in the 1980s shows that the industry expanded massively, to make Los Angeles the leading garment-producing city in the country. It did so partly because Mexican illegal immigrants were available to do the hard work. But this in turn greatly expanded the complementary native jobs – as foremen and managers, skilled workers, designers, specialist producers of buttons, zips, threads, dyes, fabric treatments and packaging, trucking to carry the output and so on. Insofar as the INS was able to arrest illegal immigrants and expel them from the country, this would *increase* native unemployment, not the opposite. Piore (1976) sums up what seems to be the real picture:

> Heavy emphasis in public policy discussions upon the competition between native and foreign workers is misplaced. Foreign workers are coming essentially to fill the jobs which native workers have rejected. To the extent that these jobs are critical to the functioning of industrial society – and, while there are exceptions, the jobs taken as a group do seem to be critical – the aliens are complementary to native workers and to domestic consumption patterns. Any wholesale attempt to end migration is therefore likely to be exceedingly disruptive to the operation of society and to the welfare of a variety of interest groups within it.

Furthermore, immigrants in many countries create more new businesses. In Britain, for example, the 1991 census shows that 13 per cent of British-born people ran their own firms, compared to 15 per cent for ethnic minorities, and 42 per cent of businessmen from ethnic minorities employed workers who were not from ethnic minorities. In many cases, these are businesses which would not otherwise exist – for example, Indian, Chinese, Vietnamese and

Italian restaurants, ethnic grocery shops and food factories and retail outlets. Furthermore, they often produce goods and services which, if they were not produced locally, would have had to be imported – in the garment and shoe industries, for example.

In sum, far from immigrants stealing native jobs, they immensely expand the number of jobs available for natives to do. They expand the output of the economy and provide goods and services that would otherwise not be produced – to the loss of all.

This is not much consolation if you are one of the people who lose their jobs. But economies are in constant change with the rise of new industries and the decline of others. Immigration is largely irrelevant to this. Indeed, immigrants make it possible for declining industries to survive longer and so sustain jobs for natives. But immigration is a small element in the overall supply of workers, far smaller than other increases that have taken place. Consider what happened to France when Algeria became independent in March 1962 and about 900,000 French people who had lived there streamed home. By the end of the year, in the areas of southern France where the newcomers settled, unemployment briefly peaked at 20 per cent. But it declined quite quickly over the following months to 6 per cent, and then 4 per cent a year later, the same as the national level. Or take, the return of the Portugese colonialists from Portugal's former colonies in Africa (Angola, Mozambique, Guinea Bissau) in 1977–8: the numbers were equal to about 5 per cent of Portugal's population, but there was no increase in unemployment in the medium term. One hundred and twenty-five thousand Cubans fled in the spring of 1980 to Miami, part of nearly a million fleeing there over the decade. The city's workforce increased by about 7 per cent, but there were no effects seen in local unemployment levels. Or take the 'baby boomers', the surge in American births after the Second World War when the servicemen returned home. In the late 1960s and early 1970s, when these children were old enough to start work, there were four million added to the workforce – but without any effect on the unemployment rate. The same is true of the immense number of new women workers who took jobs in the 1960s and 1970s. If men had followed the same logic for women workers as legislators did for immigrants, presumably they would have tried to get a law preventing women going to work.

It seems clear that increases in the number of workers has little or no effect on levels of unemployment. The availability of workers does not determine how many are needed. That is decided by how many consumers want the goods or services the workers produce. The expansion in the number of consumers – which is what happens with an increase in immigration – expands the whole economy and so the number of jobs. Indeed, some people have seen increased immigration as the way to expand the economy and reduce un-employment. The only reason that immigrants are attacked on the issue of jobs is not because of any economic effect they have but simply because they are foreigners – and they provide, especially illegal immigrants, an easy scapegoat.

Other opponents of the immigration of unskilled workers have attacked the problem from exactly the opposite angle. The availability of cheap labour, they say, keeps alive industries which should be shut down in the interests of modernisation. Presumably imports would be required to make up the lost supply. In this case, if there are competing native workers, they are eliminated with the immi-grants. This argument was employed in Singapore to try to eliminate backward industries. It did not work, and the government was obliged to backtrack. More troubling for the general argument is the knock-on effects of the employment of natives in complementary activities – the losses could be far higher than any possible gains.

Or, a different argument: if cheap immigrants were not available, employers would be forced to modernise equipment, improve productivity and raise wages to recruit native workers. This wildly overestimates the freedom to manoeuvre of employers. Almost certainly it would require higher prices, tending to make the industry uncompetitive. Only by restricting competing imports from abroad would it be possible to make this work. We have already seen the argument of British farmers that seasonal migrant workers are needed to gather the strawberry harvest – and without this, imports increase. An alternative would be to ban strawberry imports, charge higher prices from the captive local market and pay the workers more. Leaving aside the clash with all the other external obligations of the government (and access to foreign markets for the rest of exports) that would mean less strawberries would be eaten due to the price, and the poor would be deprived. More often, without immigrants, the industry would just close, imports would increase and unemployment would rise. Where services are at stake, they would simply no longer be available. For example, working mothers with dependent children would be forced to pay more for childcare or give up work.

But should immigrants be brought in to do the jobs – dirty, dangerous, ill-paid – which the natives refuse? Here the hypocrisy is extreme. To insist on protecting someone's welfare by not allowing them to work when they are willing to, the work needs to be done and people gain both in the country where the immigrant works and where he or she is from, is perverse. Unemployment is the deal offered to avoid lousy work! One might as well argue that native workers should be less educated so that they would be willing to do the lousy jobs. Of course, allowing people to work at these jobs does not justify poor pay and conditions. But the campaign to improve pay and conditions for the worst-off workers is separate from denying them the right to work at all. In the same manner, in the past, it would have been intolerable to prevent native workers working at these jobs in the interests of protecting them.

None of this affects those ambitious politicians who blame immigration for unemployment – the connection is 'commonsense'. It is an ancient charge – perhaps the populist leaders of classical Rome raised the same accusations against foreigners coming to the city. Certainly, the charge is common wherever there are migrants. At the turn of the last century in Britain, the same connection was drawn, unemployment being blamed on the arrival of Jewish refugees from tsarist Russia. The same refrain occurred during the inter-war Great Depression in the US – in 'the manner of a crusade', Martinez (1976) records 'the idea was promulgated that aliens were holding down high paying jobs and that by giving these jobs to Americans, the depression could be cured'. The campaign was directed against Mexicans. Many left the country or were driven out. The Mexican-born population fell from 639,000 in 1930 to 377,000 in 1940. Yet still in 1940, the country had the second-highest level of unemployment ever recorded. In fact, expelling complementary workers may have increased the number of native workers laid off, apart from the effect of the loss of the Mexicans as consumers.

No one learned any lessons. In the late 1970s, the French government, faced with rising unemployment, attacked the position of half a million Algerians and Africans, in order, it was said, to free jobs for the French unemployed to take. By chance, a government report was published at about the same time which showed that the natives would not take the jobs if they were offered – for every 150 jobs made vacant by immigrant workers forced out of France, the native unemployed would refuse all except 13. And that was not taking into account the knock-on effects – layoffs among native complementary workers and the native unemployment resulting from expelling a significant part of the French market (half a million immigrant consumers).

In 1976, the US government began a campaign to search out and expel illegal immigrants in order, it was said, to cut American unemployment. The INS claimed that one-and-a-half million workers were arrested in 16 cities over a two-year period. The head of the INS proclaimed that if they could punish employers for giving jobs to undocumented workers, 'we could quickly open at least one million jobs for unemployed Americans'. No one held him to account for this piece of fraudulent nonsense. But as we have seen, regardless of the number of jobs 'freed', there were very few American takers.

This dispiriting failure did not deflect the government's instincts. In the early 1980s, the Reagan administration launched another drive to arrest illegal workers in nine major cities. But again few Americans wanted the jobs when they found what the work was like – the minimum wage (then US$3.25 an hour) for a ten-hour shift on heavy and dirty work.

Destroying the nation

The fears about a fundamental change in a way of life as the result of the arrival of foreigners come close to the panic at 'being swamped'. But the fears are not just of one type. They cover an immense range – from a frustrated rage at the treasonable 'betrayal of the nation' to a mild sense of unease, fears about being unable to communicate or find friends. Not only is the range wide, the fears are very unevenly spread among people. It has often been noted that fear of foreigners tends to be greatest where there is least contact with or knowledge of them – eastern Germany with fewest immigrants is the stronghold of the most fervent anti-foreigner organisations in the country. With less knowledge or contact, it is possible to turn foreigners into a threatening fantasy rather than individual people, men and women with names and unique faces.

The problem of the threat of foreigners is not a function of evidence one way or the other. The fears are interwoven with misty concepts about identity – the idea of the 'social homogeneity' of a people, of common values or cultures, of national identity itself. It is quite unclear why we all have to be the same, and why, if we are not (as in fact is the case), it should be a problem. The ideas are usually so subjective that almost anything passes – they miss the rocky terrain of what passes for the facts and can allow individual prejudice free rein.

The fears are real enough even if they are difficult to make specific or assess. Some of them relate to the existence of the modern state and the loyalties it calls upon. What people fear is being taken from them is not only a way of life, but a government, the power to protect or order the way of life. As we noted earlier, the modern state took over many of the attitudes of family, tribe or clan: the fierce hostility to and suspicions of outsiders; a spiky sense of national honour and intense sensitivity to insult; the ferocity of response and unquestioned obedience to the institutions of collective power. The family is supposedly a line of common descent (the tribe and clan less so), so that membership is exclusively by birth. Nobody without that descent can join it, an idea embodied in the nationality laws of a number of countries, notably Germany and Israel. In reality, nations are quite unlike families, since they are far too large (and past mixtures far too great) to pretend to anything except a fictional common descent – they are necessarily mongrel rather than pedigree. In practice, different biological descents are reduced to the more superficial element of skin colour or some other physical feature.

Insofar as foreigners migrate, settle and have families, a common culture increasingly supersedes the idea of a common biological descent – or at least raises difficult questions. The idea of a black German or Englishman may in the short-term challenge attitudes in a way that a black American does not. But as the idea of a common culture comes to define the nation, it makes it possible for anyone to join. Europe is in transition, learning slowly the changing nature and mixture of a culture that descends from many traditions – German Turks, French Arabs, British Indians and an immense number of other combinations are slowly becoming part of the unity. And although black Americans are a fundamental part of the US, Americans are with equal slowness coming to accept many other denominations – American Ethiopians (or Ethiopian Americans), American Yemenis, American Afghans and so forth.

Those on the extreme political right wing resist these adjustments as an unacceptable dilution of the privilege of nationality. But it cannot now be argued in terms of race. It is 'culture' which has been used as the code word for 'race' (meaning skin colour). When British Conservative Enoch Powell launched his inflammatory assault on immigration in 1968, he did it, he said, in defence of a British 'culture'. When Margaret Thatcher, then leader of the Conservative opposition, in 1978 sympathised with the feelings of British people that they might be 'rather swamped', it was by 'people of a different culture' (as we noted earlier, people from the 'New Commonwealth and Pakistan', the code word for 'black', were four in every 100 of the British population at that time, a bizarre spectacle of swamping).

On the surface, the culture argument is weaker than the racist one. If the basis of the British nation is a common culture, it can be joined by outsiders. Indeed, over the last millennium, immense numbers of outsiders have joined. However, this is true also of those with different skin colours. The late Bishop of Stepney, Trevor Huddleston, once demonstrated that the proportion of London's population which was black in 1790 – largely slaves and servants – was the same as in 1980; and yet all disappeared into the larger population.

The xenophobes have a stubborn belief in the 'cultural homogeneity' of the nation, its common values, but as suggested earlier this is largely myth. What is in common is a much narrower range of things – language and state being the most obvious. If we were to take the word 'culture' seriously then it would seem immensely varied – by locality, origin, class, dialect, religion, inheritance and the individual combinations of this variety. Furthermore, this package is in continuous change, so that we can hardly say what the

Frenchman of 2000 has in common with the Frenchman of 1900, let alone 1400 or those long millennia before even the concept of France was invented. Even over a ten-year period, the cultural change is often remarkable. In daily life, we take the changes for granted and they pose no necessary problems. Immigration may add an additional component of change, but far less than local norms will reshape immigrant perceptions. The Glaswegian Pakistani becomes a perfectly valid variation, and contrasts with the London Pakistani. The combinations provide new charm and enrichment without any intrinsic potential for conflict or alienation.

One element of cultural melding is intermarriage. Figure 2 gives figures on this for a selection of countries. Projections for the US suggest that people with more than one 'national ancestry' will increase from 18 million in 1995 to 81 million in 2050. Psychologists have agonised that those born of parents from different countries or 'cultures' produce forms of psychiatric disorder in which the child does not know 'who they are'. Yet this happens without 'mixed' parentage, and does not happen to most people of mixed parentage. The diagnosis gives priority to nationality in the formation of individual identity, so that those who are of mixed origin do not know to which state they should be loyal, an idea perhaps more revealing of the prejudices of the psychologist than the patient. Similar worries are sometimes expressed about 'somatic identity' – skin colour. Consider the anxieties of a Canadian government expert in the 1970s:

> A person's identity includes a sense of one's body. This in turn is determined not only by one's physical traits but also by socially provided standards and ideas with regard to what is physically normal, fit, beautiful, clean and pure...Of particular interest in the present context is colour and other physical characteristics used in a group or society to define racial identity.

The meditation concludes that the 'mixed marriage' (by Canadians of different skin colour) 'frequently' leads to children with 'a confused somatic self-image', since 'not knowing where they really stand with respect to accepted norms is anxiety-creating'. This piece of humbug is presented as a serious case. Thus does ancient bigotry, without evidence or common sense, masquerade in the new garments of pseudo-science.

In practice, at least some of the children of mixed marriages delight in their position. It gives them a privilege over the population at large who can claim only one line of descent: the freedom to choose their ethnic identity, rather than have it thrust upon them. Choosing in this way can produce some odd outcomes. In the 1980 census, 40 million Americans claimed to be of Irish descent, a far greater number than could possibly be descended by natural increase exclusively from the four to five million Irish that migrated to the US.

Assimilation, racial and cultural, is so clearly apparent in almost all developed countries that it is perverse to suggest it is impossible or rare, let alone that it threatens the nation. All those Poles who became Germans (before 1914) or French, the Italians who became French or British, just like all the others who became American, are marked now only by their names (unless they have been changed) and perhaps a few fragments of the past: a photograph, a letter, a grandmother's ring. In some cases, the quarters where the immigrants first lived – the Chinatowns, Little Italy, Old Jewry and so on – seem to leave more traces. But the second generation has usually moved on, absorbed into the population at large.

Antisemites have had a vested interest in arguing that Jews are peculiar in that they resist assimilation and therefore are a permanent alien force – dedicated in the more extreme forms to taking over whole societies. The notion is so fantastic, it is extraordinary that it could even temporarily have captured the minds of otherwise sane people. We do not know how many Jews down the ages became gentiles, nor how many gentiles – in the interest of marriage or occupational specialisation – became Jews, but we have no reason to think the numbers small. Those that stayed in countries for longer than one generation and were not legally restricted rapidly sank into the local culture – the German Jews were German, until they migrated to Poland and became Polish, until they migrated to America and became of the essence of American identity. On the other hand, the religious and political disunity of Jewish populations is equally impressive, ranging across the board of modern beliefs, from Karl Marx and Sigmund Freud to the Hassidic groups. The idea that this diversity hides a single conspiracy is an heroic defiance of all evidence. The only token of separateness, of an unwillingness to assimilate, is that some continue to call themselves Jewish. But then some call themselves Welsh, Breton, Bavarian, Tuscan or Texan without demonstrating an unwillingness to assimilate.

In practice, as we have noted earlier, the surges of sudden alarm at 'swamping the nation' are orchestrated by the political leaders of the centre. No matter how intense and even frightening at the time, they turn out to be temporary steps along the perpetual road of reshaping peoples. They are dangerous for the establishment only when they coincide with major social and economic upheavals of a scale not seen in Europe and North America in the period since the Second World War. Much more impressive in the developed countries has been the absorption – and subsequent assimilation – of immigrants and the reshaping of nations.

Public services: are there free lunches?
Competition between natives and newcomers is not just about jobs. There is also competition for public services – for housing, places in hospitals, clinics and general practices, schools, and for welfare benefits. One of the favourite accusations against immigrants, specially illegal immigrants, is that they exploit these public services without paying for them, they 'live off welfare', or in the language of the British tabloid press, they are 'welfare scroungers'. Indeed, both government and press suggest immigrants enter the country, not to work but to live off welfare services. They are robbing the taxpayer.

So strong is the belief in the US that immigrants live off the welfare system, and that this is a heavy burden, that different levels of government have tried to exclude them. California's Proposition 187 was directed to stop government funds being used to finance welfare benefits for illegal immigrants (the Proposition was struck down by the courts as unconstitutional because it denied education to US citizens, that is the US-born children of undocumented workers). The 1996 Federal Act forbade immigrants to use federal programmes for a period, and the 1997 budget extended this for the first five years in which an immigrant lived in the country. Six states introduced other measures to block immigrant access to public services, and tried to sue the federal government for the costs of immigrant use of services.

The idea of immigrants living off welfare benefits is simple and straightforward. But trying to prove it is ferociously difficult, if not impossible. To start with, what are we to include in public services? The US system includes welfare and social security, Medicaid and Medicare, and public schools – but also the police, fire protection, public health and defence. Distributing the costs between users of these complex programmes is difficult, especially because the government borrows to pay for some of them – the costs are off-loaded onto future taxpayers. In addition, a calculation of the costs and benefits cannot be valid just at one moment, since the system assumes contributors pay in some years of their life and draw benefits in others – the costs are heavy for the young (in education) and the aged (for pensions and health), low for working adults. So adults in the working age groups pay for the young and the elderly, and are paid for before and after they leave work. To assess the costs and benefits means taking at least a life and a half to test net payments and net subsidies (and assuming that there are no changes in the system, when almost invariably there are).

Immigrants are, in general, concentrated in the working age groups, so, like natives in the same age groups, they are major contributors, drawing very little in benefits and subsidising everyone else. As they produce children or become old and retire, as with the natives, their contributions decline and they start drawing benefits. So it is the age structure of the population which is the most important determinant of contributing and receiving. For example, one calculation suggests immigrants in the US on average pay US$1,800 more in taxes than they receive in benefits. But if their US-born children under 20 (being born in the US means they automatically have US nationality and are thus not immigrants) are included, the big education costs mean they pay US$370 less than they receive.

In the US, the biggest programmes of the federal government in the 1990s were social security and Medicare. These are over-whelmingly used by natives, not immigrants, largely because of the age of the immigrants (and recent elderly immigrants are not allowed to use them for five years after arrival). Immigrants are said to benefit from Medicare to the tune of US$404 per year, compared to US$269 for non-immigrants, but if provision for the elderly is included, the total social security benefits for non-immigrants rise to US$3,800.

However, the differences in net contributions vary much more between different immigrant groups than between immigrants and natives. Those from Latin America and Africa, including many of the low-paid (so paying less direct tax and getting more State transfers) and those with big families (using more of the education system) receive more than they pay, whereas for Asians, Europeans and Canadians the position is the opposite.

With regard to illegal immigrants, the picture is much better for the Americans. Although they may not pay direct taxes – they do pay indirect taxes on what they consume – many, as single workers in the working age groups, draw almost nothing from the system. Through their indirect tax contributions they subsidise everybody else. However, the more children they have who go to school, the more they draw benefits indirectly.

In terms of unemployment benefits, immigrants tend to draw relatively little, since they are in general in the most active and employable age groups (so often they have high rates of working, up to 90 per cent). But this depends on booms and slumps, the rise and fall of employment. When there is a recession, it may hit hardest those parts of the economy which employ many immigrants – in the clothing industry, farming, construction, heavy industry and so on. Rates of unemployment may be temporarily higher for immigrants than natives, but, as anyone who has had to live on unemployment benefits knows, this is far from 'living off welfare'. The figures may be complicated in some countries by the nationality laws. As mentioned earlier, those descended from immigrants in Germany remain 'immigrants' (unlike in the US), and the familiar problem of large numbers of young people without jobs, especially among unskilled workers (which is what many immigrants are), swells the numbers. But what seems to be the high unemployment rate for immigrants is in fact youth unemployment.

The picture is hideously complicated, so there is no easy answer. But the common suspicions seem to be wrong. Given the age of immigrants – like the natives in the same age groups – they subsidise the rest of the population until they have children or become elderly. More important, welfare systems are nowhere so generous as to allow easy money, especially for foreigners – nor of a level to influence the decision to migrate. 'Welfare scrounging', people drawing benefits while also working, may be a general problem in the country as a whole, but it has nothing to do with immigrants as immigrants. It is a red herring in the discussion.

One distinguished European expert on migration (Böhning, 1974) once presented the issue in this way:

> There is a lot of talk about the 'problems caused by migrants' – that it costs money to house them, to school their children etc – as if these problems would not arise if the labour were of national rather than foreign origin…If there were no migrants, there would be few of the problems attributed to them; but there would also be fewer of the goods they provide which enhance the welfare and comfort of all residents.

The social damage of immigration

At a lower level than the heroic accusation of 'destroying the nation' there are innumerable petty criticisms of immigrants and immigration, so many that only a few can be examined here. One accusation is that immigrants choose to segregate themselves in separate areas and so fail to assimilate. In fact, the notion of groups living in separate localities of the city is as old as the city itself. Leaving aside the cases in which people were forced to live separately – as with the Jewish ghetto – living together for any group has immense benefits. It also allows a concentration of shops which sell foods eaten by particular ethnic minorities sharing a common language, religious and social welfare institutions, of clubs for ethnic groups and many other services, including banks from the country of origin, cinemas showing films from the home country, libraries with books in the group's mother tongue. If there is hostility from the wider society, living together offers a measure of security. Just as the abandonment of particular jobs by the natives offers the unskilled immigrant the chance of work, so the abandonment of areas of poor housing gives the opportunity for immigrants to replace them. These concentrations sometimes last more than one generation, but usually only if there are continuing new arrivals of immigrants from that ethnic group – for example, in New York's Chinatown. Without this, more commonly, the children of the original immigrants, having now become in all important respects natives, move out, often to better-off localities that are not marked by any particular ethnic minority. The better off the descendant of the immigrant, the more likely that they will live in areas marked by level of income rather than ethnic origin. Assimilation is, again, a matter of time – unless the ethnic character of an area proves a commercial attraction, as, say, with Little Italy in New York or Chinatown in London. Some of the better-off children of immigrants now run what have become much more expensive restaurants.

However, the experience has not persuaded governments against pursuing dispersal policies for refugees, to 'relieve the pressure' on the facilities in big cities and encourage assimilation. The US government tried to spread around the country the Cuban refugees of the 1960s and the Vietnamese of the 1970s; the British government is at present pursuing the same policy with asylum-seekers, making their welfare benefits dependent upon them living where the government directs them to go. Of course, it may be too generous to attribute the British motive to a wish to encourage assimilation. Dispersal may just be part of a general package to produce the greatest misery among refugees, to discourage others from trying to enter the country. The experience is that the places to which the refugees are sent do not have the facilities to cope with them; the degree of racism and physical violence is high; and as soon as possible the refugees move back to where friends and relatives live, as it is easier to get work and housing. Dispersal is just an additional oppression in the lives of refugees. More importantly, what is to the benefit of the refugees is to the benefit of society – the creation of ethnic quarters, with a distinct culture and restaurants, enriches the rest of society and helps the tourist trade. It is the differences which enrich, not that preoccupation of chauvinists, the uniformities, the cultural 'homogenisation'.

Some have argued that there are special difficulties in absorbing a population which speaks a foreign language. There are obviously additional costs in education to provide language or remedial classes for the children of immigrant parents. This is true only for the first generation of immigrants, and of no greater significance than accommodating all special needs in education. There are similar problems in inner-city schools in the great diversity of languages spoken. But what can be a serious problem in educational administration can also be a great enrichment of the education which the students give each other. It is hardly an argument against immigration *per se*.

What about the absorption of those of a different language and culture into work and business? People of the same language and culture, it is said, interact easily, the 'transaction costs' are lower. This has appealed to some economists and theorists of 'social capital'. Where the costs are high – foremen cannot understand workers and vice versa, businessmen and women cannot do deals easily with each other – this may reduce economic activity. This may be true, although the role of ethnic and religious minorities in trade for thousands of years might lead one to doubt it. But the interaction is seen only as negative, without attention to the possible benefits of a diversity of ethnic groups, stimulating innovation. Is this not once again the lurking beast of xenophobia, this time hiding behind the econometric algebra?

Immigration also becomes tangled in local fantasies about hygiene. Immigrants are accused of carrying diseases, although they are no different from all travellers in their potential to transmit infections. They are accused of living in dirty conditions. Of course, work in poor conditions at poor pay (reduced further if much of the income earned is sent to families in the original home) encourages higher levels of ill-health, but this is true of the poor generally. This is an occupational or public-health problem of low incomes, not something specific to immigration. As always, the only reason for criticising immigrants on this score is because they are foreigners, whereas the real reason for the problem is because they are concentrated in poorly-paid jobs.

Immigrants have always been accused of committing a lot of crime. In the past, it has reached extreme levels – in 1859, 55 per cent of those arrested for crimes in New York were Irish-born, and a further 22 per cent were immigrants from elsewhere. But the crimes were in the main trivial and the arrests may just have reflected police prejudice (like the high level of arrests of young blacks in many cities). Proper surveys contradict the prejudice, showing immigrant rates of crime are generally lower than native. In Germany in 1970, for example, the crime rates for Italians, Greeks, Spaniards and

Turks were under half that for Germans. Of course, the foreign contacts of some immigrants may make easier international crime, and the rise of foreign criminal gangs can be seen in many places.

In the US, Mexican (and formerly Colombian) immigrants have played a key role in smuggling narcotics, just as between the wars in the Prohibition era, Italian immigrants or their children, the Mafia, grew rich selling illegal alcohol. The Chinese triads, and now Russian gangs, have a similar reputation. But these examples are as remote from the experience of ordinary immigrants as East London's famous English gangsters are from the mass of the British population. It does not take foreigners to invent or sustain crime.

Some in the Green environmental movement have produced a different argument against immigration. More people will take Australia or the US, the two countries in which the case is most popular, beyond its 'natural carrying capacity'. A shortage of water and fertile land make it necessary to prevent increases in the number of people. However, most Australians and Americans do not depend on the supply of water or fertile land for their livelihoods, and the existing population densities of the two countries are far below much of the rest of the world. Both countries are rich enough to buy both water and food in the world at large if they need it, so the domestic supply is not decisive. In a global context, these are problems of a relatively minor significance. But, again, one suspects the argument is used only because immigrants are foreigners, not because they present some special danger.

The ingenuity and diversity of arguments against immigration and immigrants are impressive. Like the proverbial hydra, no matter how many heads are cut off, the monster instantly grows new ones. It suggests that the arguments do not matter. It is the state of mind producing the argument which is important – blaming foreigners. 'Foreigners' and 'natives' are abstractions, because no particular individuals are involved. You may not like Lucy, who is a native, and like Carlos, who is a foreigner, but that does not affect the abstract argument. The argument is really about national identity, about who you are, not about people you know. That, in turn, is not a static condition. The identity of people is interwoven with numerous insecurities, pains and fears, all real enough, but without any relevance to whether people are foreigners or not. Immigration, especially as presented in the occasional deluge of misinformation which passes for public debate, provides a hook on which to hang an immense number of discontents. If immigrants did not exist, it would be necessary to invent them, to create scapegoats. A few years ago, the Japanese became much taken with the idea that a Jewish conspiracy was destroying Japan. There was a flood of books and articles showing once again that the bankers of New York and the Communists of Moscow were conspiring to secure the downfall of the country. The argument was all the stronger because there were no Japanese Jews – or at least none publicly known. The need for the argument was greater than any credibility. Chronic silliness often seems to have a life of its own.

4 — Why Countries Need Immigration

The truth is that normal migration automatically regulates itself

Meyer London, US Congress, 1914

The previous chapter examined the arguments for controlling immigration. In general, it found them weak, certainly too weak to justify general control. This chapter looks at the case for increased immigration.

The need for unskilled workers

Each country's workforce is composed of a mix of skills, competencies and experience; a complex of interdependent aptitudes. It is in a state of constant change as technology and people's demands change. Public discussions of education and training usually concern only the highly skilled and the system that produces them. It is here that the worries about scarcities are debated. This is understandable, since the skills are rare and costly to produce. But at any one moment, a large number of workers are, in one sense, 'unskilled'. Yet this unskilled workforce alone makes it possible for the skilled to work. Without it, there is no economy and no high productivity.

'Unskilled' is a very primitive term – and a changing one. Just as the migrants to America are vastly better educated than in the past, many of the modern unskilled workers in the developed countries would have been accepted as skilled a century ago. As we have seen, 'high-school drop-outs' are about 10 per cent of the American labourforce today, but only 30 years ago, constituted 40 per cent. A century earlier being a high-school drop-out would have been a major step up for the majority, who were hardly literate and hardly finished primary school. In the same way, as we have seen, emigrants from developing countries are drawn often from the minority of the better educated, some of them having degrees, and yet often do the lowest-skilled occupations in a developed country. All this shows is that someone is unskilled or skilled relative to local standards.

Governments around the world try to educate their populations to higher and higher levels. Everybody in developed countries today attends secondary education, and what would have been seen as extraordinary numbers some years ago continue to university or college. Education is seen as a key factor in how much you earn, in the competition between countries, in expanding the economy and in making everyone better off. But the 'unskilled' jobs do not disappear, although they may be radically reduced. In a developed country, higher educational levels steadily reduce the local supply of workers willing to undertake the unskilled jobs. The educational qualifications of those looking for their first job may not be spectacular, but they are sufficient for them to feel, with reason, that they can find better work and better pay than that offered. A welfare system which gives some minimal level of livelihood, or families willing to support unemployed adult children, makes it possible for young workers to refuse the worst jobs and wait for better ones. They are increasingly over-qualified for the jobs on offer. In time, some workers give in and accept jobs which are below their qualification level – in an important sense, their qualifications are wasted. In many developing countries, the same problem arises – there is an over-production of the educated relative to the number of jobs available.

The pay that people earn in the two cases – developed and developing countries – is, however, set by local norms, not international ones. The weekly wage of the 'low paid' in a developed country is often unbelievable riches in a developing country. Given this major income difference, it makes sense for the educated worker in a developing country to try to take a job below that which matches his or her formal qualifications in the place where incomes are highest, a developed country. It is partly a distorted decision, since the cost of living in the developed country is much higher and there are many other disadvantages arising from the high cost of labour. But in general, workers do well by migrating.

The persistence of low-skilled and low-paid jobs in the developed countries is remarkable. The obsessions with the skilled make this mass of workers apparently invisible to official society, a mass of non-people. Take the British case. In 1990, it was estimated that there were some 10 million low-paid workers in the country (as measured by the Council for Europe's 'decency threshold', workers receiving 68 per cent or less of average full-time earnings). In the late 1990s, this level of low pay was closely related to the quarter of the population said to be living in poverty (up from 14 per cent 17 years earlier). The same is true in other developed countries, and is likely to be true in the future. In projections of the American workforce, a study for Congress forecast that about half the jobs on offer in 2050 would need only a high-school diploma or less – in personal service jobs, cleaning, construction, security, retail sales and so forth.

The 'unskilled' are, as we noted earlier, a very mixed bag, including those, in fact, with a wide variety of 'skills' (even if these are not officially recognised). Workers are willing to accept some jobs and not others. This accounts for the existence of high rates of demand for workers in some jobs and high unemployment in others. Congressman de la Garza expressed his frustration with this in 1978, when unemployment was a severe problem in the US:

> In Washington, you see 'Help Wanted' in every restaurant and every Macdonald's. Everywhere you go, you see 'Help Wanted' [even though] we know there are countless thousands of aliens illegally in the Washington area, apparently all with jobs.

Consider the problems of eastern Germany. At the time of the reunification of Germany, the exchange rate between the currencies of the two parts of the country was set at 1:1 (before unification, it had been around 20:1). This made eastern German wages very high indeed relative to the prevailing levels of productivity. Ten years later, two million workers had moved to the west in search of work, the eastern workforce had shrunk by a third, and still one million workers were unemployed in the east. Yet as we noted earlier, German employers were desperate to bring in Polish immigrants to work either on long work permits or as daily commuters. The government refused most of the requests, and as a result the economy stagnated. There is a chance that if the German government had allowed in more Poles, the whole economy would have been lifted and German unemployment would have ben reduced. As it was, economic stagnation stoked up the most ferocious anti-Polish and anti-foreigner xenophobia.

Young workers not unreasonably, assume that with their education, they should not be forced to take the worst jobs. In New York, in the mass of small garment-making factories in the high-fashion industry, there is always a desperate shortage of workers, as in its equivalent in Paris, the cellars where Turkish illegal workers make clothes. But taking a job here means a ten-hour day of furious piece-rate work, in dark and dangerous conditions (cold in New York's winter, suffocating in high summer) for pay which, in the 1980s, was US$1 an hour (the federal minimum wage was US$3.35). In the eyes of many, it would have been suicidal for any native-born son or daughter with ambition to get trapped in such work.

Yet, as we have noted, the sweated trades are often vital for the economy, vital in allowing the highly skilled to work. Without the army of cleaners, laundry workers, porters, waiters and helpers, the rest could not last for long. Nowhere is the case more clear-cut – and often more painful – than in the case of highly skilled or pro-fessional working mothers. Childcare is a precondition for them being able to work. Yet maids and nannies, the 'unskilled', are usually the target for exclusion under immigration controls. The Singapore case (Appendix IV) illustrates this, the government simultaneously urging graduate women to have more babies and making it impossible for them to get the home help required at an affordable price.

We have better information on the dependence of the US on unskilled or semi-skilled immigrants than that of Europe or Japan. In the six leading states to which the majority of immigrants head, three-quarters of tailors and waiters, 78 per cent of cooks and over half of taxi drivers and textile and garment workers are immigrants. Immigrants make up 18 per cent of the Los Angeles construction workforce. In farming, especially harvesting, as we have seen, the dependence has always been heavy – in Washington State, 70 per cent of the employed in the peak harvest time are said to be illegal immigrants. The same was true of Kentucky's tobacco crop. 'The strong economy,' the *Financial Times* (23 February 2000) commented, 'had given Kentuckians choices better than sweating in the tobacco fields'. For the US as a whole, one estimate has it that without a ready supply of illegal workers, fruit and vegetable prices would rise by at least 6 per cent – without allowing for the stimulation to imports that higher domestic prices would encourage.

The implications were recognised by others. On 5 May 1985, the *Wall Street Journal* pointed out that 'Throughout the south-east [of the US], the idea of a life without illegal immigrants is as alarming as the idea of life without the rays of the sun'. The INS wrily recognised that government rhetoric and government policy were not in accord: 'The actual policy of the US government is quite different from its stated policy, which is the strict control of the border and strict restriction on entry. The *de facto* policy is to keep the door half open' (INS commissioner Lionel Castillo, testimony to Congress, 1989). In 2000, the head of the Federal Reserve Bank, Alan Greenspan, went further: without more immigrants, inflation was likely to bring to an end the long boom in the US economy. Immigration served as a 'counter-cyclical' factor, damping down the forces that produced recession. No wonder some Americans were confused – hating immigrants but finding them crucial to economic success. Figure 3 shows the close parallels between flows of migration and the general fluctuations in the economy for a different example, Switzerland.

There may be less information for Europe but some does exist. By the late 1960s in Germany, for example, 45 per cent of immigrant workers were employed in manufacturing, and three out of every five in the country's key export industries, engineering and chemicals. About 29 per cent had jobs making cars and trucks (compared to 6 per cent of Germans) – the heart of what was then Germany's spectacular export performance. At Ford's Cologne plant, three quarters of the workforce was Turkish (over half of Cologne's Turkish workers were at Ford). In the 1980s, half the miners and half the refuse collectors were immigrants, and it would have been impossible to operate the national railways without them, let alone most of the hotels, restaurants and cleaning services. Stuttgart City Council carried out an exercise to asses the effect of the city losing three-quarters of its immigrant workers. The conclusions were that public transport and services, like the construction industry, would be brought to a halt; schools and nurseries probably could not function; unemployment among the German workforce would soar; and the quality of life for everyone would deteriorate rapidly.

Without immigrant workers, manufacturing could go abroad to where the workers were cheaper, but the mass of services for the people of Stuttgart would have to stay local, even if at much higher cost. W.R. Böhning (1974), the well-known researcher on migration, put it in this way:

> You cannot transfer a coal shaft to somewhere in Turkey simply because labour happens to be abundant there; the solution is also irrelevant for the large number of building workers; you cannot build the houses needed in Frankfurt in Sicily; nor is the proposition applicable to migrant workers in private services, domestic goods, public transport or other public service occupations: if dustbins need emptying in Munich, the workers for the job must be found on the spot.

The period from the 1960s to the end of the century was, in the developed countries, one of increasingly tight controls on the immigration of unskilled workers and of increasing promotion, through education, of native workers. Without the support of unskilled workers, this will lead to increasing unemployment of the natives. The impact of this growing crisis has only been softened by increasing illegal immigration – with all the resulting cruelties, miseries and injustices that increased official control inflicts on the unskilled migrant worker. As we shall see in the next chapter, this crisis is going to get very much worse.

Controls do not work

The debate about controls, which began in the 1960s and 1970s in Europe made immigration an issue. In doing so, it trapped governments in a xenophobia of their own making – it became increasingly difficult to follow economic common-sense. As we have seen, in practice the issue was less about the arrival of newcomers – white immigration of skilled and professional staff continued, and there were always other big exceptions. It was about the black and brown workers who sought unskilled jobs. Controls were necessarily discriminatory both in terms of race and class – the poor black or brown unskilled worker was the target.

Numerous other abuses followed. The behaviour of immigration officers at consulates abroad and ports of entry, the increase in deportations, stop-and-search tactics by the police (with many more arrests of blacks than whites), the atrocious mistreatment and arbitrary detention of refugees, and the constant attempt to deny the validity of their claims are only the more obvious results. The institutional structure is more oppressive than individual prejudice – but individual prejudice and the racists assaults that go with it also rise and fall with waves of official hysteria about newcomers.

The confused signals of the political establishment are the cause, on the one hand seeking to present an image of fairness, justice and compassion, on the other trying at almost any cost to stop the arrival of the unskilled. Officials responsible for carrying out immigration policy are put in a corrupt position – not making money out of their victims, but defrauding them of their rights.

Yet the system does not work, and cannot be made to work at a politically and economically acceptable cost. Migration controls work in a rough and ready sort of way only in certain kinds of regimes – in the old Soviet Union and its Eastern European allies, in China and Vietnam – with some important leakages – in Nazi Germany. They still work in North Korea and Myanmar, but poorly so. They do not work where the basic livelihood of the population depends on an open economy, on increasing transborder flows of goods and people. The administrative controls required to police these flows make the flows impossible, and this is economically disastrous. The only way left to reduce illegal migration is to try to deter the migrant with a control regime so fearful that he or she will not make the attempt at entry. So far, the deterrence has not worked, and it is not clear that it can ever work since the numbers of people who do succeed in crossing borders without papers is more impressive than the number who are stopped. Whatever the dangers and costs, people persist. The tighter the controls, the higher the price of labour and thus the greater the incentive to break in. If the immigrant is successful, he or she benefits, and so does the country as a whole. But the greatest beneficiaries are the smugglers, strengthening through this activity other illegal transborder trans-actions – the movement of narcotics, of stolen goods (particularly cars), trafficking in women. Thus, the very attempt to impose order on borders reproduces chaos, the very disorder that governments are supposed to fear most.

Illegal immigration is the invention of the law. Seeking to end it has nowhere been fully successful, but it is least successful for open economies with a strong demand for unskilled workers and few on offer. The political and economic costs of effective control are far too high. In practice, governments are obliged to be hypocritical – to wave a big stick, make periodic heroic statements of being tough and implementing a once-and-for-all 'crackdown', impose regimes of deliberate brutality on the minority of migrants who get caught and an unintended cruelty on many more who are damaged or killed along the way. Without dragging illegal migration into the open, making it legal, there can be no attempts to prevent the cruelties and the deaths, let alone tackle trafficking. Keeping unskilled migration clandestine is a policy of tolerating crime and a regime of intended or unintended brutality. As we have seen, the asylum order is itself corrupted by the attempt to end illegal immigration, and the compassion supposedly reserved for refugees is turned into its opposite, a crippling hostility. And yet, in the end, governments are forced to issue periodic amnesties to the un-documented. Was there ever such an indictment of an absurd policy as periodically suspending it to allow a brief moment of reality to catch up?

The transformation of cultures

Migration is not simply about the movement of workers. It is also about the transfer of what economists call 'human capital' – skills, talents, experience, abilities. Indeed, it may be that all sorts of capacities are released by migration itself, which could explain why some famous migrant communities, such as Jews, Lebanese and

Armenians have such a disproportionate share of talent. Through its successive transitions, the community accumulates and cultivates exceptional ability in a range of fields.

People conventionally think of human capital as formal qualifications – having a degree in medicine or mathematics. This has been an important factor in the migration of professional workers and scientists. Think of the great enrichment of cultural life in Britain and America as a result of the flight of German Jewish refugees in the 1930s, and the flight of people from what was the Soviet Union and its allies and from China after 1945. In the hard sciences, in the professions, engineering and architecture, in music and drama, migrants have been a powerful force in advancing the quality of work in the countries in which they have settled.

In the US where, unlike Europe, it is respectable to be of immigrant origin, this is clear. Between a quarter and a third of all Nobel Prize winners who are either American citizens or residents are foreign-born (the figure is between 22 and 27 per cent for those who are American citizens). Over a fifth of the membership of the National Academy of Science is foreign-born. If we include the children of immigrants, the score is very much higher.

Something similar occurs more generally for skills, though we have only random observations of this. Thus, one in four teachers of physics in the US are immigrants, one in five medical doctors, just under half of health technologists and over half of women political science teachers. Indeed, it seems Americans are abandoning some professions. By 1985, over half the assistant professors of engineering under the age of 35 in American universities were foreign-born. In the second half of the 1980s, over half the doctorates in engineering were awarded to students from developing countries, as well as 48 per cent in mathematics, 32 per cent in business studies and 29 per cent in physical science. Given the efforts to recruit such students to settle in the US, some of these professions will become overwhelmingly dominated by those of foreign origin.

The same seems to be partly true of the newest information industries. Appendix VI shows the key role played by Asians in America's crown jewel of advanced technology, Silicon Valley. Again, including the children of immigrants would exaggerate this position even further. The role of these foreigners partly explains the changes in US immigration policy, with a deliberate attempt to recruit software programmers from the rest of the world to make up for the failure of the local supply to expand quickly enough.

It is more difficult to track immigrants in Europe. Indeed, the different culture of immigration may well lead people to conceal that they are of immigrant origin. However, there are some small indications – as, for example, the fact that the English Premiership in football employs nearly 200 foreign-born players and the English team is coached by a Swede; the English cricket team is coached by a Zimbabwean; and the British Lions rugby team, by a New Zealander. In business, the number of foreign chief executives in the largest companies has grown immensely – British Airways, Marks and Spencer, Barclays Bank, Pearson. Just under a quarter of the doctors practicing in Britain are from ethnic minorities. At the other end of the scale, two-thirds of independently owned shops are owned by members of an ethnic minority – along with a quarter of those employed in restaurants, and more than a quarter working in London transport (when some 7 per cent of the total population is foreign-born).

However, there is also the enrichment of the experience of those in many more unskilled occupations. This is more difficult to detect but may be more important if more unskilled migrants return to their original homes and work or start businesses there. This is discussed below.

The development of the world

The benefits of migration – gains to the migrants and to the country to which the migrant travels – are well established. The losses are to the native workers who lose their jobs to the new arrivals, and to the country from which the migrant comes (a subject to which we return later). In the first case, as we have seen, the losses are small because it is relatively rare that native and immigrant workers are competing (unlike the situation for skilled workers) and more than offset by the overall gains to the country concerned. In the second case, the losses are partly offset by remittances, payments made by workers who have migrated to their families left behind.

Thus, in general, it seems that the world gains through the easy migration of workers, and loses when controls prevent this happening. There are few studies that assess the pattern of gains and losses, partly because the assumptions to be made to cover the gaps in knowledge make it all a bit arbitrary and artificial. Hamilton and Whalley (1984) made one of the few studies of what an ending of migration controls would have meant for the year 1977. They calculated world output would have gained by between US$4.7 billion and US$16 trillion; world output was valued in 1977 at US$7.8 trillion. So, in terms of overall world development, the effect of ending controls ranges from a small addition to world output (ending controls would add 0.6 per cent) to trebling it (or 205 per cent). If the higher estimate is anything like the truth, immigration controls impose a major sacrifice on the peoples of the world. It is a burden borne disproportionately by developing countries.

However, remittances are some small compensation for this loss. Even under current constrained conditions they have become important for some countries. The total remittance flows from developed to developing countries at the beginning of the 1990s were reckoned to be between US$34 and US$66 billion, with an annual average in the previous decade of US$700–1,000 per worker. These are informed guesses, and certainly an underestimate, since they have to exclude payments made outside the official banking system (legal and illegal) and payments made in the form of goods sent or carried by returning workers or through trade.

At the other end, remittances have become very important even in the official figures for a number of developing countries (see Table 11). For example, in Bangladesh (1977–8), payments from its workers abroad equalled 56 per cent of the country's export earnings and over half of government revenues. In the case of Egypt in 1993 – with many of its workers working in the oil-producing Middle East – worker payments to their families were half as great again as export earnings; for Jordan, 83 per cent; Morocco, 53 per cent.

Remittances, like worker emigration generally, used to get a bad press in developing countries. To have to go abroad to work was seen as an indictment of a country's development efforts, a failure to be able to employ people at home, and robbery by other countries of the labour resources which ought to be developing the country.

This was most extreme in the case of the 'brain-drain' in the 1960s and 1970s, when the cost to developing countries was put at extraordinary levels. In the 30 years up to 1990, North America is said to have absorbed over one million professional and technical staff from developing countries, a total loss, according to the US Congress, of around US$646 million. In the 1970s, Africa lost about a third of its most skilled workers to Europe; in the last half of the 1980s, about 60,000 middle- and high-level managers fled the continent. Sudan lost 17 per cent of its doctors and dentists, a fifth of its university staff and a third of its engineers; Ghana lost 60 per cent of the doctors trained in the early 1980s.

If we think of the world as no more than a set of countries which own their population, then this does look like theft by the developed countries. But that would be a foolish way to see it. The loss of skilled and professional workers on this scale is as much a vote of no confidence in the government concerned as a flight of capital. It becomes more like a flight of refugees, a flight from spectacular misgovernment, from appalling working conditions and pay levels often so low that they are below subsistence. The remedy is not to end the right to work in developed countries but to make an environment at home in which people want to stay and work.

The same school of thought that saw the brain-drain as theft disapproved of remittances on the grounds that these payments went to feed workers' families, not to develop the country. This is an odd criticism because it cannot be a bad thing if workers' families are better-fed, and if in being so increase demands on, say, farmers to produce more food, and thus the farmers order more equipment and other inputs to farming, and so on; that is a general expansion in the economy. In any case, many other things are accomplished from remittances – as the two diagrams on Bangladesh and Thailand in Figure 4 show. Many families are accordingly able to lift themselves well above the local average level of income.

In the late 1970s, Mexican illegal migrants to the US were said to send back about US$2 billion per year to their native central states of Mexico (or four times the revenue that the Mexican tourist industry was then generating). By 1999, the total inflow of remittances from Mexican workers in the US was put at US$6 billion (or equal to over 1 per cent of Mexico's GDP). The flow affected family incomes for about a fifth of the population, and was the most important source of income for 70 per cent of the families of migrant workers. A different study in the mid-1980s put the total flow at between US$1.5 billion and US$2.5 billion, most of it going to the slightly better-off rural families in the poorer areas of the central states of Mexico (where over half the men aged 20–40, said they worked regularly in the US). Furthermore, another study calculates that for the expenditure of every dollar received and spent in Mexico in remittances, there was a further US$2.69–3.17 expenditure as a multiplier effect (that is, the sum total of spending as the dollar was spent in one transaction after another) – a maximum total of US$8 billion.

Of course, remittances fluctuate, especially from workers in the oil-producing countries, where the numbers of workers employed varies as the oil price fluctuates. People are critical of this, arguing that it makes long-term development efforts more difficult because revenues are unstable. For example, official total remittances fell by 60 per cent for India between 1974 and 1976, and were halved between 1982 and 1986. But these fluctuations are no different from the price changes that affect raw material exports. To say that because what exports earn varies widely a country should stop exporting altogether, would be absurd – it would be, to use an English expression 'cutting off your nose to spite your face'.

For migrants, there were disasters, and the nationalist press in the developing countries concerned often played on these to suggest that workers should not – or should not be allowed to – migrate for work. But there were many more successes, which is why people continued to try to emigrate. The largest houses (and those built in brick rather than mud) in the villages belonged to families with a member working abroad. Whole villages in the Fuzhou area of north-eastern Fujian in China, in Kerala or Jullundur in India, or North Ilocos in the Philippines, or the north-east of Thailand or Sylhet in Bangladesh boomed. Increased incomes supplied the families with consumer goods – the cooking stove, the refrigerator, the colour television, the small car or motor cycle – and with new steel ploughs and small tractors for the farm. Remittances paid for the setting up of new small businesses (with a taxi, a truck or a bus), for the education of children, for marriages and medical operations.

Families began to take a period of emigration for granted and to build it into the life plan of one or another child, to build it into normal expectations. Emigration was preferred, planned and anticipated with excitement. And it advanced the whole household. As a Philippines Minister of Labour commented in 1985 (against those deploring emigration): 'Overseas employment has built more homes, sent more children of the poor to college and established more business enterprises than all the other programmes of the government put together'.

How very much more could be accomplished if there were no immigration controls? It might then be that the scale of transfers through work could become the main route for development, for the conquest of world poverty. Or to turn the argument round, immigration controls in the developed countries impose very heavy costs on the developing countries, and the heaviest is the failure to shift world poverty. The UN (UNDP, 1992) made an esti-mate of what this cost might be, putting it at a minimum of US$250 billion per year. Another study estimated the cumulative loss to the world of US$1,000 billion up to the year 2000. What would happen, the UN asked, if immigration controls were removed? If 2 per cent of the workers of developing countries moved to work in developed countries and earned no more than a poverty-level wage of US$5,000, they would earn a total of US$220 billion. Perhaps they would remit to their families in developing countries US$40–50 billion annually, or US$200 billion over five years. This would be vastly larger than either aid or investment flows, and with strong multiplier effects outside the existing centres of development.

This is an artificial exercise for many reasons, but especially because it relies only on the results of a transfer of remittances. It was suggested earlier that most migrants have little wish to abandon their homes and go into permanent exile in a foreign country. They do so only to get access to work. But given immigration controls, the price of secure access to work is settlement, giving up one's homeland and nationality, and trying to get citizenship as a defence of the security of the job. With free movement between countries, there would be no need to change nationalities or seek foreign citizen-ship. There could be continual circular migration, work abroad as the need arises, for a season, a year or longer. Furthermore, without controls, it is likely that more of the skilled and professional workers would opt either to return to their homeland or to circulate, transferring both assets and knowledge. Both countries, source and destination, would then gain.

Migration then becomes not a simple transfer of a worker from one country to another, but the circulation of human capital. To some extent, this already happens. Koreans in Los Angeles also operate businesses in Korea and circulate between the two. The computer engineers and software programmers that the Taiwanese government attracted home from California (to a special science park, Hsinchu) also operate both in Taiwan and the US. The case of Silicon Valley suggests this could be part of a broader pattern in which several points around the globe interact in the advance of the information industry, interact with capital, with know-how and with labour.

Other schemes are operating to attract home the skilled emigrant. The Chinese government is trying to copy the Taiwan example by attracting home the 50,000 Chinese students who chose to stay in the US after the massacre of Tienanmen Square in 1989. They have now become important in advanced American industry. The Indian government's Non-residential Indians scheme has had the aim of encouraging Indians abroad to invest in India and perhaps return to start new businesses. Various other governments maintain similar schemes. But none of them will work if the domestic political order fails to facilitate all this new business and technology, fails to provide a reliable energy and transport system, a reliable system of law and order.

Governments the world over want to tie down their scarce skilled workers, want to oblige them to settle and accept the overriding authority of the government. So a world of circulating workers is very unsatisfactory to governments, not least because the state income depends upon being able to tax an immobile taxpayer, not catch him or her in movement. The instinct of governments is to discourage international mobility. Nonetheless, return migration strengthens the forces of reform and facilitates a world in which the gap between developed and developing is increasingly crossed and ultimately closed.

This concerns only the highly skilled. But in terms of basic development, the unskilled – or what passes for unskilled in a developed country – is probably more important. The man or woman who uses the savings from working abroad and draws out of their experience of this time sufficient knowledge and confidence to start a small enterprise – a restaurant or a garment business, a small taxi or truck firm, a language school or travel agency – is more important for the local development effort. With major circular migration, economic development could be speeded up more effectively than anything that currently goes under aid programmes.

In sum, then, the greatest damage of immigration controls is inflicted on developing countries and their capacity to use their labour forces to greatest advantage. Perhaps the greatest opportunity for the eradication of world poverty lies in opening up the labour markets of the developed countries to workers from the rest of the world.

Disarming the xenophobes

The past three centuries of the history of Europe, and latterly the world, have been dominated by states and the associated question of nationality: the government to which one owed loyalty. Steadily the world was colonised by states, excluding all who were stateless. Some peoples, like the Jews, found themselves marooned by the closing of borders, suddenly stateless. When established governments chose, the former great strength of the Jews, their cosmopolitanism, turned into a terrible weakness, a target for persecution. Nationality came to define a person's identity, to internalise the imperatives of state interests. In the twentieth century, when men were required to be willing to die in war for their state, nationality became even more important.

In mythical terms, nationality was: sacred – a matter too important to be discussed, let alone changed or chosen; egalitarian – the collectivity of the nation formed, supposedly, a band of equal brothers and sisters, without classes, tribes, clans or indeed families; democratic – even in despotic tsarist Russia, the nationalists portrayed the monarch as leading the nation by the popular will; socially consequential – it makes a big difference whether you are a member of one nation or another; the newspapers daily stress the misfortunes of being a foreigner; genealogically continuous – the nation is, again, like a family, biologically descended from the same group, racially distinct.

The degree to which all or any of these myths were accepted varied with the country and the time. But, for example, they defined the passport as a high and sacred document, a fundamental declaration of an individual's political vocation and primary loyalty. To lose it was an act close to treason. The xenophobic were only extremes of the norm – and often applauded by moderates. The principle of the state was hostility to foreigners, those who were defined as necessarily loyal to another state and therefore an actual or potential enemy.

Global integration and the spread of cosmopolitanism makes many of these features of the old order not just comic but dangerous, especially when married to aggressive racism. As we noted earlier, racist incidents in eastern Germany are not just a sad illustration of a lack of civilisation, they affect Germany's potential to attract foreign investment and skills. Rocking the boat when there are so many in the crowded waters threatens all. Those most closely associated with global integration – apart from the officials of one or other state – find the issues fading. Nationality is becoming no more than a legal convenience (or inconvenience), the passport an irritating necessity to make international movement easier (but still very much more than irritating if you do not have one). Similarly, where people want to live becomes, again, a matter of convenience rather than profound loyalty.

Governments are in two minds about the process. On the one hand, the economic power of the country and the livelihood of the population (and hence the political survival of the government) depend upon continued economic integration with the rest of the world. On the other, integration seems to undermine the instinctive loyalties on which governments depend for political survival, the payment of taxes, and also, if the need arises, to fight wars. Most governments from time to time depend upon shameless appeals to chauvinism, and elections are fought on which party will best protect the nation, not on how best to administer a fragment of a world economic order. Governments are not averse to railing against foreigners and international entanglements at the same time as doing everything needed to collaborate with foreigners and strengthen entanglements with them.

The liberalisation of foreign trade was the first great transition (1950–1980 and beyond), and of capital movements the second (1980 onwards). These processes reflected and speeded integration, the creation of a single world economic system. Although neither process is anything like complete, the third and greatest transition, the freeing of people to move, has hardly begun. It crystallises the confusion, the two minds, of governments – between the needs of the economy, embedded in a global system, and the local political order, embodied in the popular vote of the citizens. The German scheme of the 1950s and 1960s, the *gastarbeiter* system, tried to separate the economic question, the need to import workers, from the political, who should be allowed to settle, to have the rights of a citizen. The *gastarbeiter* had the right to work temporarily, but without the right to settle. It might have worked if it had not been embedded in a system of growing restrictions on movement. The temporary worker had an interest in making his or her access to work secure, and the only way of doing so was to attain the right of permanent residence (the Germans did not at that stage allow immigrants German nationality). So the temporary workers strove to become permanent, to accept exile – *gastarbeiters* became immigrants.

The central political problem in immigration control is not the relatively rare xenophobic mass action of the population, nor even the daily racist incidents, assaults and discrimination. These can be shocking and horrifying but are usually relatively brief and the causes are not always what one might expect. For instance, in France in 1973 nearly 50 Algerian immigrants were murdered in Marseilles, leading the Minister of the Interior Marcellin to declare: 'We have to expel foreigners who disturb civil order. Many people perceive the government as taking a response to violent incidents by expelling the cadres of the immigrant organisations.' In fact it turned out that the core of the outrages was an attack launched on Algerian gangsters by French gangsters who wanted to restore their control of the narcotics and prostitution rackets in Marseilles. The French gangsters employed the extreme right-wing National Front to give a political cover to the attack.

Of more permanent danger is the ambivalence of governments, with one foot in the politics of xenophobia, the other in a world economy. Xenophobia is intrinsic to the old order of states and the reality of warfare between them. In practice, the natives have adjusted to the changing ethnic and cultural composition of the population far more smoothly than governments. In the US, it is not immigrants that are in general the target of horrifying racism but some of the oldest Americans of all, the black American population. Many people in America and Europe, especially the majority in the cities, have embraced, indeed exulted in, elements of cosmopolitanism, in food, music, dance, culture generally, and in the emergence of new blends, Turkish German, Indo–British, Franco–Arab and so on. Given the awful traditions in both Europe and America, no complacency can be tolerated about the persistence of racism and xenophobia, especially if there were a general social and economic crisis, but there are no grounds for deep pessimism. According to the latest census, California no longer has a majority of Anglo–Saxons – and despite grumbling, disputes and surges of hostility, this has been achieved with remarkable smoothness.

This shift in popular perceptions has taken place, as we have seen, with little political leadership. Indeed, the leadership has been on the other side, demanding the impossible, an end to all immigration and, in some cases, 'repatriation' (or exile for those born in the country to which their parents or earlier ancestors migrated). Established European governments have been more accepting of xenophobia than willing to acknowledge the real role of immigrant workers in making possible the native standard of living. Accommodating xenophobia has been the chosen means to divert people from embracing extreme right-wing political options. Yet this is to feed xenophobia, to make racism respectable, and to keep the issue of immigration on the boil.

Accommodating xenophobia has built a prison for European political leaders. A policy of no immigration has served as a substitute for thought, a knee-jerk reaction, for three decades. Even as the world economy is clamouring at the gates, moving towards more common-sense is fraught with danger. So great has been the official misinformation on the subject – and the toleration of the lies of the popular press – for the peoples of Europe to learn that they depend and will increasingly depend on immigrant workers provokes a shock of disbelief.

However, populations are more sensible than is allowed. Remember the outbreaks of racism in the 1960s and you can see the change. The film of Enoch Powell, making his notorious 1968 speech, thundering, enraged, apocalyptic, has become slightly risible with the years, a psychiatric tantrum that is amazing in a mainstream politician: how could he have made such a fool of himself? The irrelevance of those fears, nightmares, is a mark of the passage of time. It is now not unrealistic to see many of the ideological trappings of the old nation-state being dismantled without causing a crisis to people's sense of identity; loyalties being shunted into the less dangerous area of football, or becoming attached to regions or cities. But until the political establishment finds the courage to speak the truth, the process remains vulnerable to the political adventurer riding on public ignorance.

Conclusions

Even without considering the future, which is what we shall do in the next chapter, the positive arguments for ending immigration controls are strong. The size and composition of the workforce is inadequate to maintain an expanding economy. This is most clear in developed countries in terms of 'unskilled' labour; there is an immense shortage, and this causes higher levels of unemployment in the native workforce. Furthermore, if the right to work in unskilled jobs were extended to the rest of the world, the flow of resources to developing countries – in remittances from their workers abroad and in the human capital of returning migrants – would be of an order far beyond any existing scale of transfers. This would raise the prospect of a serious attack on world poverty. Finally, a globally integrating economy is refashioning the countries of the world, displacing the old position of the state and its ideological companion, xenophobia. Immigration is the last frontier here, the last major obstacle to the emergence of a single world, a world without war.

5 — The System Collapses

Over nearly three decades the political parties in Europe relied on the simple proposition that primary immigration had ended, would not be resumed, and had probably been a mistake in the first instance. In Japan, it had never been officially started. In North America, it was grudgingly accepted. The European governments responded to periodic surges of xenophobia (as often as not initiated by government or opposition panics, supposedly at being swamped by foreigners) with 'crack-downs': increased controls, increased arrests, increased deportations. Then, at the beginning of the new century, in an astonishing turnaround, they went into partial reverse. Without explicitly admitting it, they are by implication driven to recognise that the system they have constructed is auto-destructive. It threatens the competitive capacity of each country, and so the very livelihood of their citizens – which in turn threatens the political survival of the government itself.

It is a quite extraordinary reversal, accomplished without explanation as to the past ruinous record, indeed without even acknowledging the stupidity of the preceding policy regime. The change is taking place without, so far, strangely, the xenophobic reaction of public opinion which had for so long been supposedly the justification for immigration controls. Why have governments suddenly grown so brave, brave enough to lead the citizens rather than represent only the minority of chauvinists? This chapter attempts an answer to this mystery.

Of course, the change is still very far from full liberalisation: establishing the freedom of all to work where they wish. It is 'cherry-picking' – trying to recruit from developing countries their best and brightest, with a shameless disregard for the development priorities of those countries. Western aid organisations remain dedicated to the development of developing countries ('the eradication of poverty') at the front door, while home ministries try to steal one of the means to develop, those countries' skilled labour, at the back door. But it is a chink in the walls of the fortress, and raises far wider issues than can be comfortably kept within the narrow framework of national self-interest.

Of course, there had been straws in the wind. When Hong Kong began its moves toward rejoining China, many governments sent teams shopping for skilled workers there – New York telephone companies trawled for telephonists, the airlines for pilots, Singapore, Canada and some of the Central American republics for anyone with professional skills. Some of the Europeans, for example the British, without fanfare were also recruiting more broadly, mainly white professional workers, but some black as well. Subsequently, as we have seen, the US expanded the issue of visas to attract more skills. Australia moved in the same direction, but then Australia's businessmen had always argued that increased immigration produces a boom.

But in Germany in the 1990s, it seemed that opinion was still moving in the opposite direction. There was growing opposition to continuing the constitutional right to settle in the country accorded to those who could prove German ancestry (who were 'ethnic Germans'); this despite the fact that those who qualified for this right were younger and therefore lowered the average age of Germans (4 per cent of 'ethnic Germans' were over 65, as opposed to 21 per cent of Germans proper). On the other hand, the then-leader of the Social Democrats, Hans-Ulriche Klose, argued that, in the light of population projections for Germany, the country needed 300,000 immigrants annually to shoulder the tax payments required to finance the growing pension burden of the increasing numbers of elderly. And the Free Democrats provocatively identified the contribution of Germany's non-German workers as 10 per cent of national output and DM90 billion in taxes and social contributions.

They were minority voices, cutting against the grain of the conventional wisdom. There were still no consistent champions of immigration in most countries. When the yellow press went hunting for 'bogus asylum-seekers', it seemed to reflect the real state of opinion, violently opposed to foreigners. That persisted until, unwittingly, the American government launched a world competition for skilled labour, a kind of worker arms race.

The scramble for skills

The long boom in the US economy in the 1990s produced a great scarcity of workers. Not only did unemployment reach levels that used to be thought impossible, and without the raging inflation expected to follow from such a scarcity, but the welfare rolls emptied rapidly and illegal migration supposedly soared. There was considerable pressure to allow in more unskilled workers (see Appendix II).

However, this did not provoke major concern from the government. This only came from the pressure of employers keen to be allowed to recruit more skilled workers from abroad, vital, they said, if expansion was to continue. As we have seen, immigration law had been shifted in the direction of recruiting scarce skilled workers. The 1998, allowance for temporary visas for the highly skilled (H-1B visas) seemed to be exhausted earlier and earlier in the year. The numbers were consequently raised to 115,000 for two years, followed by 107,500 for 2001 and 65,000 for 2002 (half of them reserved for IT specialists). Silicon Valley employers complained that even this was not enough. They said that in the middle of 2000 there were 340,000 vacancies in IT in California, and 850,000 skilled vacancies as a whole. There were demands in Congress for the numbers to be lifted to 200,000, or even 250,000. In the event, in October 2000, Congress lifted the numbers to 195,000 for three years, the visas valid for three years with a further three-year renewal possible. In the last year before the increase, just over half were for computer industry workers, 13 per cent for architects, engineers and surveyors, and 8 per cent for managers and administrators. Some 43 per cent were granted to people from India, 10 per cent to Chinese, 4 per cent to Canadians and 3 per cent each to British and Filipinos.

Advanced skills – or at least, graduates (56 per cent of H-1B recipients have no more than a bachelor's degree) – are one thing. The discussion about skills is becoming interwoven with the more general problem of the declining size of the workforce. Projections suggest that the number of US workers will start to fall absolutely from 2010. The implications are immense, but painfully so for government finances. The doubling of the number of those aged 65 or more up to 2050 means a steadily heavier burden of finance on a shrinking number of workers, potentially leading to both a rebellion against the tax system and the bankruptcy of the social security and Medicare schemes.

The US bid to capture a bigger share of the world's skilled workers threw down the gauntlet to everyone else. US companies, armed with the easing of visas, recruited globally – not just from the familiar sources of India, China and the Philippines, but among final-year students in Mexico, Brazil and Argentina. Canada and Australia moved to revise the points system by which they chose immigrants in order to admit more temporary residents skilled in the handling of computer software. The competition pulled in others – from South Korea, the Netherlands, Ireland, New Zealand, Singapore, Norway and so on. Western Europe, with a supposed deficit of 600,000 skilled workers (which, according to the European Commission, would reach 1.6 million by 2003), began to seek recruits in eastern Europe, the Ukraine and the former Soviet Union, as well as in Asia. The Irish were said to be particularly energetic in recruiting in Bulgaria.

In the spring of 2000, German employers argued that industry lacked 300,000 skilled workers. No doubt such demands had been made before and resisted. But now, it seemed, the US and others would capture the lion's share of the world's supply if Germany did not make a bid. The German government, a Social Democratic coalition, finally moved – 20,000 work permits were to be issued over two years, directed particularly at software programmers 'from India and Eastern Europe'. The first visa was ceremonially awarded to an Indonesian software specialist on 1 July after 5,000 applications had been received.

The German proposal was modest enough, particularly when compared to the American initiative. But it still provoked hostility among the Christian Democrat opposition. The opposition candidate in the North Rhine–Westphalian state elections, as we have seen, countered the government with the slogan 'Kinder staat Inder' – 'educate German children, not import Indians' (the British Conservative opposition employed the parallel slogan for British children). The candidate lost. Furthermore, pressed by business to allow the foreign recruitment of skilled workers, the Christian Democrats were obliged to backtrack. Party leader Friedrich Merz accepted the need 'to move the focus of our policy away from those who need us to those whom we need'. Thus was the xenophobic competition which so often dominated the discussion of immigration and asylum at least temporarily suspended. But no permanent quarter was to be given in the pursuit of power – Merz has threatened to make immigration an issue in the federal elections of 2002.

Meanwhile, the Indian press carefully reported both the slogan 'Kinder staat Inder' and the rash of savage racist incidents in eastern Germany (an Indian scientist was assaulted in Leipzig) to illustrate that Germans were dangerously ambivalent on the question of Indian immigration; in turn, the German government warned Germans that unless they could put their house in order and end racist incidents, Germany could not compete. Xenophobia was now becoming economically disastrous in the new world order.

The twin threads of the story – the need for high skills in global competition with other powers, and the need for low skills to protect the welfare of the population – activated the debate in Japan. By tradition, the Japanese government has been exceptionally suspicious of and hostile towards foreigners and immigration (and also to the ethnic minorities of Japan). So the rather modest measure of 1996 (Employment Counter Measures Plan) to admit people with skills or cultural accomplishments not available in Japan is perhaps more remarkable than it appears on the surface. The projected shrinking of the labourforce has long been known. The UN projects that to stabilise the working population to the year 2050, 609,000 immigrants would be required annually (by the final year, a third of the population would be of foreign origin). Saga Prefecture sweetly did its bit and introduced a dating service to encourage more marriages, and so hopefully more Japanese babies.

The debate within the government is strong but unresolved. The Ministry of Justice is said to favour a proposal put forward by the employers' federation (Nikkeren) to admit legally unskilled workers to replace the army of illegal immigrants who do the jobs the Japanese have abandoned – jobs which are one of the three 'K's – *kitanai* (dirty), *kiken* (dangerous) and *kitsui* (hard, difficult). There are also other specific shortages. To expand the health system to cope with the increase in the aged population will require a doubling in the number of nursing assistants over five years to one million. But the pay is so poor, it is said, that only a third of the half-million Japanese who take the training subsequently work at the job. The Labour Minister opposed allowing immigrants to take the jobs.

However, the American and European scramble to capture some of the Asian supply of high skills provokes more urgent worries. The Japanese Ministry of International Trade and Industry (MITI) estimates the shortage of IT engineers at 200,000. There is discussion of a proposal for all Japanese children to learn English, so that they can from an early age learn to surf the web. And when Japanese Prime Minister Yoshiro Mori visited India in August 2000, his first stop was at Bangalore, the centre of India's IT industry, to appeal to Indian programmers to migrate to Japan where, he said, venture capital was abundant to help them start new businesses. Fortunately for his Indian hosts, he did not try to sign up his audience; just before his visit, Singapore Prime Minister Goh Chok Tong had done just this to the staff of the company he was visiting – 'like someone invited to dinner trying to hire the cook', as his host put it. The Japanese government is well behind in the field, trapped in that mixture of political and economic imperatives that produces paralysis.

In the British case there has been remarkable progress, particularly given Britain's reputation – from the behaviour of its football sup-porters and its yellow press – as one of the most xenophobic countries in Europe. The hysterical hostility to asylum-seekers seems now to have become a corner set aside by the government for the free expression of xenophobia, while the government tries to make real changes in the work-permit system, to allow in many more people with scarce skills. The changes were becoming necessary, the government said (but without elaboration), as 'a response to crisis or widespread dissatisfaction with the current arrangements'. They would admit, the government said, 100,000 foreign (non-EU) workers in the year 2000, would remove restrictions on foreign students at British universities seeking work, and allow in workers with only an occupational training diploma. The changes are expressed with shameless self-interest (and without reconciling them to British aid policy) – 'to put Britain at the front of an international scramble to attract "wealth creators"' (Minister of State, Home Office).

The measure is still modest, the first half of a promised review which will introduce more radical changes. What is more remarkable, however, is the change in tone.The Europeans did not restrict themselves to the electronics sector. In July 2000, Italy's Social Affairs Minister, said: 'Our country badly needs a larger labourforce.' Reports from business associations across the north of the country said it was impossible to recruit workers in heavy industry, construction and agriculture. Udine requested 4,800 immigrant-hiring permits, but was awarded only 1,000. The Social Affairs Ministry, which handles immigration, said that 15,000 slots for sponsored immigrant workers had gone in the first morning they were made available. Italy's official rate of unemployment at the time was nearly 11 per cent.

British Home Secretary Jack Straw, on a trip to India, proclaimed that his government wanted 'to actively celebrate the diversity of Britain'. His deputy, Barbara Roche, declared her aim to be 'to de-stigmatise the term "economic migrant" and present overseas workers as an asset to the economy'. Whatever had successive governments been doing for three decades to establish this stigma firmly in the public mind – most recently in the debate about 'bogus asylum-seekers', who were thoroughly stigmatised as, the government said, really economic migrants and criminals? Few in the government retained the capacity to blush at the wretched record they were now supposedly 'adjusting'. Roche now called for 'a grown-up debate' on immigration, as if all the previous ones had been infantile. With endearing innocence, she observed:

> In the past, we thought purely about immigration control. We need to think now about immigration management…by having X workers from abroad, [it] might release a bottleneck that allows 10 UK citizens who are currently unemployed to [get work].

But had that not always been true? There is no new shortage of skills in Britain – the skill shortages officially recorded between 1988 and 1990 were nearly 80 per cent larger than that in the year 2000.

For the moment, the broader issues remained on one side. However, the *Financial Times* saw the opportunity and stated:

> the focus should not be on the most skilled. Fears that underqualified migrants will swamp national identities are exaggerated. History teaches us that economic migrants…invariably make up for any short-falls with their dynamism.

But the newspaper did not raise the issue of asylum-seekers as one possible source of workers. Of course, asylum-seekers might not have the rare skills the government thought it needed, but they might fill many of the roles the newspapers identified. Here the government had no interest; it insisted on the lack of any relationship between the two issues and reaffirmed yet again with leaden inevitability and the customary lack of evidence – 'Procedures are being increasingly misused by those who have no real fear of persecution'. Where official compassion is at stake, persecution is the appropriate response.

Reports from India suggest that few potential migrants are as impressed with the British offer as with the opportunity to join their numerous friends in California – where green cards so often lead to American passports (even if the new American citizen wanted to live in India). In any case, it is not clear that foreign demands can be met even partially by Indian supplies. With 1999 employment in India's IT sector at 280,000 and output doubling every 18 months, the IT workforce is projected to be 2.8 million by 2008.

In fact, the discussion is dominated by the old order of separate nation-states, grabbing whatever they can. But the global organisation of the industry is changing. As shown in Appendix VI, the world industry straddled many countries, integrating Silicon Valley and numerous points in Europe, Asia and Latin America, with workers travelling between these points, staying for given periods (Indian programmers stay in California on average for between three and five years), but not necessarily remaining permanently anywhere. Such a pattern fertilised many points in the industry. There was not a one-way flow from developing countries to California, but simul-taneously a reverse brain-drain too. The national competitions seen so clearly in Europe, which led to countries trying to 'kidnap' foreign workers, was part of the old order in which living and working required a national loyalty. In the future, the new technologies allow for workers to remain at home – in India or elsewhere – and work for employers further afield – for example in Silicon Valley. But such patterns put the workers beyond the knowledge, let alone the control and taxing capacity, of government.

Ageing

The topic which so many governments in developed countries are still unwilling to tackle (except as a budgetary issue of how to finance pensions) is ageing and the projected decline in the number of workers. The signs have long been visible – at least from the population projections of the 1980s. Fewer children per family and declining fertility entail, in due course, fewer workers and a decline in population. By the 1990s, the rate of growth of population in the developed countries was only 81 per cent of that required to keep it stable. Spain's total population is projected to shrink by 10 million people – to 30 million – by 2050. To keep it stable, the country will need 10 or 15 million immigrants over the next half century. In 1999 Spain turned away nearly one million illegal immigrants, the number is said to have trebled in 2000. Many menial jobs which Spaniards are unwilling to do are now done by immigrants. In the wine-making and fruit-growing industries they are mostly Muslim men from North Africa.

> In the large cities Poles and Romanians have cornered the foreman's jobs on construction sites. Latin Americans and Arabs do the heavy shifting. Corner shops are run by mainland Chinese. Prostitutes are Nigerian. And yet Spaniards cling to the belief that they are and should remain a homogenous society.
>
> Leslie Crawford, *Financial Times*, 10 October 2000

Some of the sharpest declines are occurring in southern Europe: in the first half of the twenty-first century, Italy's population is scheduled to decline by 28 per cent, Spain's by 24 per cent. The EU as a whole is set to decline by 11 per cent.

The developing countries will have, over the next half century, a much younger population due to the preceding decades of high fertility, and so a workforce and population continuing to grow. As a result, the bulk of the world's young workers are increasingly concentrated there. In the last two decades of the twentieth century, over 90 per cent of the babies in the world were born in developing countries, and in the year 2000 there were over eight births there for each one in a developed country (in 1960, the ratio had been four to one). Table 10 gives 'youthfulness indicator' figures for the regions and some of the countries of the world, ranging from the most youthful, 44 in Central Africa, to –2 in Italy, and 1 in Spain and Japan.

This shift in where people are born shows an equally big change in where the world's workers live later when the infants become adults. Consider the numbers added in the last decade-and-a-half of the twentieth century:

	Developed countries percentage	Developing countries percentage
Total population:	+14	+103
Working population (15–65 years):	+6	+130
Young population (20–40 years):	+10	+108

For the US and Mexico, the comparable figures are, for the former: +26, +16 and –9 per cent; for the latter: +86, +129 and +87 per cent. The figures for Canada only exaggerate the contrast, showing that increasingly the youth of North America is going to be Mexican. The supposed great weakness of the developing countries, the 'population explosion', is emerging as their great strength for the future.

Simultaneously, as we noted earlier, the working life for each individual is shrinking. Early retirement – in Europe, workers are retiring four years ahead of the statutory retirement age on average, and some up to ten years – lops off years at the end, while increasing education lops years off at the beginning. German graduates on average enter work at the age of 28. Within two decades in Europe, the normal length of a working life for men has been cut by a third. Furthermore, even through the working years, fewer hours are worked – the average working week in Germany fell from 48 hours in the 1950s to 35 in the late 1980s. There are longer holidays and breaks for training or childbirth. It is amazing how much of this great reduction in working time has been more than made up for by increased productivity (which is itself related to increased education and training, as well as innovation), so that average incomes also grew enormously. But in sum there has been a drastic reduction in the work inputs per worker, while the number of workers has continued to grow; how will countries cope with a shrinking number of workers?

In Europe, as we have seen, in the nineteenth century, in the years of war and in the 1950s and 1960s, economic expansion invariably led to the demand for workers exceeding the local supply and, as a result, spilling out of the core zones of Europe to attract workers from abroad (as well as importing goods made by workers abroad). How much more will this pressure be exaggerated by a declining number of native workers? The livelihood of Europeans – like that of Americans – depends on their respective economies being embedded in a world economy; and it is impossible to think of contracting the economy to fit the number of workers.

The decline in fertility – the number of children per family – is only one side of the coin. The other is ageing, the increase in the number of people aged 65 or more, who are, if pensioned, dependent for survival on the contributions made by the workforce. Germany and Japan are two of the more extreme cases. The population of Germany is projected to fall from 76 to 65 million between 1986 and 2010. The population aged 60 or more is projected to increase by a half over the next 30 years, while those in the working age groups will be halved. Without other changes, this will increase the share of the average pay going to pension contributions from 19 to 28 per cent, and to health and welfare contributions from 14 to 23 per cent. The welfare of the elderly will depend upon increasing the share of the average worker's pay going to social security from 33 to 51 per cent. To avoid this, and keep the working population stable, the UN calculates, would require immigration of 487,000 annually; and to keep the ratio of workers to pensioners stable would require immigration of 3.6 million annually (and for the EU, the figure is 13.5 million annually).

In the case of Japan, with the longest expectation of life in the world and one of the lowest rates of fertility, the problems are most extreme. By 2050, the population is projected to decline from 127 to 105 million. The young age group (14–19) declined from 14 per cent of the total in 1950 to 2.7 in 1980, while those aged 65 or more increased from 5.7 per cent in 1950 to 18 per cent in 1990, and are projected to reach 25 per cent by 2025. And they are increasingly aged. Those aged over 75, as a share of those who are 65 or more, is projected to grow from 38 per cent in 1985 to 53 per cent in 2025 – with major implications for health services, since the need for care grows with each passing year. At the beginning of the new century there were four workers to every pensioner; by 2050, there will be two (the turning-point for the financing of pensions is expected in the year 2007). The same UN study estimates how many immigrants are needed to keep the 1995 working population stable, and as we have seen, projected that Japan will need annual immigration of 609,000 for 50 years.

The problem is most acute wherever population policy succeeded in reducing the rate of growth. So the same problems will affect developing countries in the future. But they have, as it were, a half century of unique opportunity to provide the world with workers. The same processes will affect the leading developing countries much earlier. In South Korea, government projections identified severe labour shortages by the end of the twentieth century, particularly in factories, mines and construction sites. Illegal immigrants partly fill the gaps – by the late 1980s, it was said that half the workers in the Seoul garment industry were undocumented immigrants. In Singapore, with its much more rigorous population-control policy, those aged 60 or more are projected to account for 30 per cent of the population by 2030. These are relatively rich countries, but the same problem is occurring in much poorer China, suffering from the severe effects of its former 'one child per family' policy. By 2030, there are projected to be between 220 and 240 million Chinese aged over 65 (or double the total Japanese population), with only the scantest means to support them.

In the developed countries, ageing exaggerates the problems of scarce workers. An ageing population buys different things – not so many household goods and cars, housing or education, and more services, large numbers of which employ many relatively unskilled workers (in medical, social and personal services, the 'caring professions'). If the shortage of workers is not relieved, it will lead to increases in the costs of hiring what workers there are to impossible levels. The burden on society of caring adequately for the elderly would accordingly become impossible. Without any other demographic changes, the quality of life for the aged must deteriorate inexorably.

A scarcity of workers is a constant theme in projections of the future of the developed countries. Clark Reynolds (1979) already foresaw for the US by the end of the century – basing his calculations on a net immigration of 400,000 – a shortage of five million workers (most of them unskilled). Somewhat later, a German study, assuming that many of Germany's factories would have moved abroad, projected 2.5 million unfilled vacancies by the end of the century, and a further 1.7 million by the year 2010. In Japan, a government-sponsored study calculated unfilled jobs at 2.7 million by the year 2000; but in the great boom of the second half of the 1980s, shortages of workers were already put at two million.

These estimates were done without the demographic data we now have. They are no better than the trends on which they are based and the assumptions made. But they show that fears of unemployment were less common than of workers shortages. Those fears may have been one of the factors behind the creation of different regional economies – the EU and the North American Free Trade Agreement (NAFTA). In the case of Europe, the 1992 intro-duction of the free right to work anywhere in the EU opened to northern Europe the workers of southern Europe (Spain, Portugal, Greece, southern Italy), either through investment there or through migration to the north. Contrary to popular fears, however, there has been no large-scale movement northwards. The admission to the EU of Turkey and parts of Eastern Europe may also go some way to creating a captive unskilled workforce for Europe's elderly. NAFTA was supposedly designed to cut migration from Mexico to the US through the development of the southern neighbour. It is not clear how seriously this was thought to be likely. The most draconian measures to stop illegal migration are embodied in the 1996 Act, the strengthening of the border patrol and the fortification of the border, without eliminating illegal migration. The long boom in the US economy proved far more powerful in attracting workers from the south than the border controls in stopping them. In the discussions which preceded the creation of the free-trade area, there was one witness to a congressional committee who saw its real relevance to the emerging US labour scene:

> As our population becomes older, the problem will not be to find jobs for people, but people for jobs. For many years, Mexico, with its relatively young and expanding population, will complement and balance our own as well as provide a formidable defence against attack on our position in world markets.

Crowder, 1990

There were other ways to try to relieve the expected shortage of workers. Extra tax allowances were offered to encourage more women and more retired workers to take jobs. As early as 1983, the US government ended any mandatory retirement age, raised the qualifying age for a full federal pension (which will rise again in the future from 65 to 67), increased the penalties for early retirement and increased the gains in pension for additional years of work after the age of 65. No doubt these changes increased the tendency for the older worker to stay at work, but they are hardly enough to affect the coming shortage of workers if the boom continues. Nor did they affect the tendency in factories to rely on younger workers – the cost of adjusting work to the elderly is too high. Japan and Singapore also offered incentives to firms to hire older workers and women. As a Japanese Foreign Office official commented delicately: 'Japanese businesses operating in an exceptionally competitive market…are generally cool to the idea of hiring women, the elderly or others with the additional costs these groups entail'. It is easier, where feasible, in pursuit of the young workers abroad to move the factories to the countries where they are plentiful.

Another possible remedy has barely been explored: persuading the aged to retire to countries where there are plentiful workers. Governments here, as elsewhere, give confused reactions. The British Exchequer tends to punish citizens retiring abroad, on the assumption that they are taking the pensions and other earnings out of the scope of British taxation, instead of welcoming the relief in costs. The Japanese at one stage, when the economy was much more robust, did explore the idea of moving pensioners offshore. 'Silver cities' were to be developed in Australia (using Filipina staff), Mexico and Spain. But it seemed the elderly refused to be separated so far from their children and grandchildren, and the scheme foundered. But it was an ingenious plan to remedy the problem, and with the declining costs and increasing speeds of air transport might become more feasible in the future.

Ageing raises in its sharpest form the problem of the supply of relatively unskilled labour. It is not that it necessarily entails the permanent immigration of settlers – the numbers required to stabilise the working population, according to UN estimates, are far too large for most countries to consider this even if the supply of migrants were available, which is doubtful. But if the aged are to be protected against the negative effects of a drastic decline in the numbers of native workers, there will have to be radical innovations.

Would governments, faced with the problem of caring for the elderly, be willing to relinquish control? Immigration controls seem to be such a powerful weapon in the armoury of national sovereignty, a key means to incite xenophobia, loyalty to the state and political support, would political parties contending to capture the state be willing to give it up? They might well try to arrange a compromise that did not blunt the weapon. Each application would then be scrutinised in detail, only those who by colour, gender, age and education conformed to a specific formula being accepted. The right of admission would be retained as the privilege of government, to bestow as it pleased, and in keeping this control immigration would remain a matter of political debate. Others might just sell off entry visas, aiming to compensate in public revenue for any loss of the right to choose. Thus, governments would organise an artificial scarcity, bidding up the price of such workers. Given that governments are no more competent at guessing the prospective demand for workers than other aspects of the economy, there would also be a large number of errors and bureaucratic complexities and delays. Employers would tend to oppose such a system because of the raised costs and delays, because they lose the right to recruit exactly what worker they wish to have.

However, fortunately the problem of ageing is common throughout the developed countries (and is already afflicting the most developed of the developing countries), so governments would be competing for workers, and the more complex and expensive the process of selection, the less likely they would be to recruit the most suitable. The balance of advantage could well operate against keeping controls. However, although the argument for free movement is a strong one, it could be that governments will still try to sacrifice the welfare of the aged to maintain their own power – unless civil society, the political opposition, affirms the primary interest of the citizens.

A servicing economy

Most people today work in something called 'services', rather than in factories, mines or farms, as was much more common a century ago. We don't make or produce things. An American economist, Richard Cooper, calculated that if you add up all those in the US who directly produce things, goods you can touch or see, it would not reach ten per cent of the workforce. The other 90 per cent produce services, everything from teaching, cleaning, security provision, the design of kitchen utensils, the driving of trucks to software programming.

Services are much more difficult to define than manufacturing, and seem to be a much more mixed bag. People have tried to construct a definition by saying that, unlike goods, the provision of a service cannot be detached from the provider. If you make cars, they can be distributed and sold by vast numbers of people without involving the people who made the car. But the provider of a service has to stand in some relationship to the consumer. A restaurant needs to bring the diners to eat (or, in a takeaway, carry the food to the eater). In tourism, consumers are brought to the provider of tourist services. For mail services, the post is brought to consumers.

The historic economy also had lots of services, but attention was mainly concentrated on the makers or providers of goods. Services were thought to be the leftovers, services provided to local consumers and hardly traded at all outside one locality – they were 'non-tradeables'. As a result, they did not form part of what was seen as the main engine of economic growth, trade. This was never completely true, as the case of tourism shows. This is a set of services that has been important for as long as modern manufacturing, and in recent decades has had an explosive rate of growth, becoming very important for many countries in generating the prosperity of the population. But there are many others. For example, if a foreign student comes to study in London or Paris or San Francisco and pays the full cost, higher education becomes a tradeable service – and the student is contributing to the export earnings of the country. The same is true for a patient who attends a hospital or clinic abroad.

However, tradeable services have now become a growing component of world trade, an engine of growth, and will continue to be so for as long as we can envisage. Indeed, manufacturing may go the way of farming and mining, becoming a marginal activity in a modern economy. But if this is so, and we accept that consumers must move to the service-provider, or service-providers move to the consumers, then the growth of tradeable services implies increasing crossing of borders and therefore increasing tangling with immigration controls and the rights of foreigners to work in another country. The problem is made even more severe when service industries involve the swift and flexible interaction between people in many different countries.

The IT industry is a good example here. Silicon Valley in California is a particular cluster of global activities. It directly involves legal immigrants, permanent and short-term, and, it is said, an army of well-qualified illegal immigrants, illegal because although they enter the US legally as tourists, they then work for the period for which their visa lasts, which they are legally forbidden to do. Although, as we have seen, the US government has made successive adjustments to try to track the illegals, they seem to expand far more quickly than the law can cope with. National boundaries, if economically effective, are increasingly obstructive to the industry. If the narrow national interests of governments were to prevail, the growth and dynamic innovation of the industry would be seriously reduced.

The IT industry involves highly skilled service workers, like other streams of workers that governments are now trying to attract – engineers, university teachers, airline pilots, medical doctors and so on. But the bulk of service workers are not here, but in trade and commerce, especially the retail trade; in hotels and restaurants; in cleaning services; portering; security; a vast array of activities which range from the highly skilled and highly paid to a mass of middle-range workers (with literacy, numeracy, ability to drive a vehicle and so forth) and the base of the iceberg, a mass of unskilled jobs that, in developed countries, are difficult to fill – except with illegal immigrants.

Changes in technology are making possible working without moving. With digital technology, people can work at home for an employer thousands of miles away. They do not have to travel to an office. Or again, medical services used to require the doctor to visit a patient or vice versa, but satellite technology is now making possible diagnosis on the web – a patient in Warsaw or Calcutta will be able to consult a specialist in California's La Jolla. But the care, treatment, nursing and convalescence will still need either the provider or the patient to move to the other. Distance learning removes the need for students to travel to universities, but it will be long, if ever, before that completely displaces the old centres of learning.

Digital technology also makes it feasible to 'unbundle' services so that the parts of the process that need many workers can be located where workers cost less. For example, data can be sent by satellite to be loaded and processed where those operations are cheapest, without requiring workers to migrate. Barbados and the Dominican Republic in the Caribbean handle US airline ticketing and the loading and processing of medical records, official statistics or library catalogues for many foreign customers. In the future, many of the labour-intensive data tasks – in population and industrial censuses, for example – could be done in those developing countries if they have people with both the educational level and the equipment. The three million criminal records for England and Wales were loaded and processed by 200 typists in Manila through an Australian contractor. Shenzhen in southern China processes the real-estate transactions of one of the largest dealers in Japan. Bombay handles the accounts and ticketing for Swissair. At more advanced levels, Bangalore, Manila and other centres in Asia and Latin America handle software programming needs for the world. Thus the service sector requires both increased migration in some areas and the offloading of service-provision to other parts of the world in others.

Similarly, while it is true – as we noted in the observation by Böhning – that the dustbins of Munich cannot be emptied in Istanbul, they can be emptied by workers who live in Istanbul but fly to Munich swiftly and are on call to move Munich's garbage. Of course, you might object that garbage management needs continuous attention and this would justify longer-term contracts allowing for Istanbul workers to live in Munich in order to be close to the work, but the principle remains. The ease and relative cheapness of fast air movement now opens up great opportunities for working without necessarily settling, without having to accept exile and a change of nationality. International contract working, pioneered for construction projects in the Middle East during the oil boom, is one way of meeting the demand for workers for specific services, but it would require the adjustment of immigration regulations.

One of the biggest beneficiaries of the opportunities afforded by air travel is one of the fastest growth areas of the world labour market – domestic services. It has had a bad press among nationalists, and there are horror stories of the gross ill-treatment of maids, but for the bulk of women involved it has provided work and incomes that would not otherwise have been possible. From South-east and South Asia (but especially from the Philippines and India, where the population has a greater command of English), the supply has been mainly to the Middle East and, before immigration controls cut off the flow, to Europe. Latin America has played the same role for North America. The workers are generally younger, fitter and better-educated than any local equivalents, if they are ever available. The people who benefit particularly are working mothers. As we noted earlier, governments in developed countries have seemed to be particularly hostile to the immigration of domestic workers, which is very perverse since there are rarely any native competitors – maids are not displacing local workers, only making it possible for many mothers to work. Canada seems to be one of the few countries to ease the entry of domestic workers and, equally important, to seek to protect their working conditions and pay.

The great growth in tradeable services opens up a world of immense opportunity for workers in developing countries – provided the legal framework makes it possible. This has not been apparent until quite recently. In the last round of trade talks between the governments of the world, held under the auspices of the General Agreement on Tariffs and Trade (GATT, which later became the World Trade Organisation [WTO]), services were included for the first time. US representatives made a strong bid to persuade leading developing countries to liberalise their imports of American services (notably in banking, insurance, IT and shipping). In effect, this was a demand to allow American executives and specialists, with their families, to set up shop for three to five years in the developing countries concerned, to live and to work there. In general, the representatives of the developing countries rejected the idea in order to protect their own banks, insurance, IT and shipping companies against the competition of American corporations. However, wiser counsels prevailed. Someone realised that the advantages in services did not lie exclusively with the developed countries. Given the grave shortages of unskilled workers there, liberalising the service trades would provide immense opportunities for work to the developing countries. The same would be true if the construction industry were liberalised, so that, for example, Chinese and Brazilian contractors could tender for highway contracts in North America or Europe. A group of eight developing countries (Argentina, Colombia, Cuba, Mexico, Peru, Egypt, India and Pakistan) advanced counter-proposals: in return for liberalising their importation of the services offered by the developed countries, the developed world must liberalise its importation of services from developing countries, changing immigration controls to admit workers accordingly.

The issue was not resolved, but passed on to the newly created WTO, but it will not go away. American, European and Japanese industries will continue to press for the opportunity to operate freely in those developing countries from which they are excluded or restricted, and in turn, companies in developing countries will press for the right to compete for contracts to clean the streets of New York or Rome; to staff hospitals in Chicago or Lille; to construct highways or housing estates in Arizona or Bavaria; to supply the staff for major shopping complexes, for restaurant or hotel chains. The pressure to liberalise is strong, and as the workers of the developed countries desert one unskilled sector of the economy after another, the lobbies that block liberalisation grow weaker. Slowly the right to work may be extended to the world.

Prizing open the state

The change in attitude towards immigration among the governments of developed countries is still remarkable, bewildering even, for anyone who had taken seriously the former policy position. In Europe, in what seemed no more than a matter of months, the old policy of 30 or 40 years standing – a complete ban on all new primary immigration – was reversed. Governments actively set out to recruit the workers their countries are supposed to need. Even more, ministers have begun to speak of the positive value of immigration, even of the newly discovered value of diversity. Of course, it will take more than a few speeches to lift the stigma that successive governments have nailed upon immigrants, but nonetheless the change of direction is slightly shocking.

The drama is less dramatic the closer one gets to the stage. There have been many escape clauses in the old order – ethnic Germans for Germany, Irish, Americans and white Commonwealth citizens for the British. The concessions are still hedged round, and the cherry-picking of the most skilled of the developing countries happens with unashamed national egotism. And the poor hunted asylum-seeker is still kept at arms' length, an object of hatred by governments, the ultimate foreigner, to be denied the opportunity to become a worker (Appendix III illustrates some of the contradictions here). But the principle embodied in the change of direction is nonetheless important. Governments are admitting for the first time that no country has a labourforce adequate to secure its future prosperity. The welfare of its citizens depends on the workers of the rest of the world, and sovereign self-sufficiency in terms of workers is a nonsense.

It is both a step towards the integration of labour markets and an attempt by governments to capture more than their share of skills, to strengthen those industries that exist within national boundaries at the expense of the rest. As suggested earlier, this contradicts the trend towards global networks, people interacting with each other in many different countries, a system that defies the control of any one government and the conception of national self-sufficiency. The advantage of the US is that its very size makes it closer to a global network than smaller powers; in the IT field, Silicon Valley is only part of a global network, so that the software programmer does not have to go into permanent exile in a foreign country, but can interact with many places. The European method is a clumsy attempt to safeguard national power, to make the industry captive within national borders, rather than allowing far greater gains by the freeing of workers to come and go as needed and accepting that dynamic domestic activity is only a fragment of the global whole.

On the other hand, increasing the supply of highly skilled professionals exaggerates the shortage of complementary unskilled workers. The potential immigrants will no doubt take such considerations into account. The support workers of Bangalore – the drivers, nannies, cooks, maids, gardeners, those delivering to the door – make the quality of life for IT specialists possibly superior there to that in Europe and North America, where such services can be obtained only illegally or at prohibitive cost. Perhaps that is why the migrants to California want to stay only three to five years, a period in which the value of the learning makes up for the sacrifices of being separated from family, friends, home and a particular quality of life.

The old system, a set of self-sufficient national enclaves of workers, has broken down. Few governments have had the courage yet to grasp the implications of ageing for the population: the necessary package of remedial measures for the problems generated by ageing – more elderly staying at work and more elderly emigrating to where the workers are available in developing countries (stimulated perhaps by developing countries competing to capture part of this relatively rich market). There will be more automation, and more activities that can be moved (as with manufacturing), pursuing the workers abroad. The liberalisation of tradeable services and construction, organised on contract, may offer some relief in terms of the need for large groups of unskilled or semi-skilled workers. But at the end, realistically, these measures will not fully resolve the problem of how to maintain the elderly of the developed countries at a standard of decency acceptable to all. That will require the development of a system of international agreement, following the models of the agreements on the liberalisation of trade and capital movements, freeing movement of labour. It will need to establish the norms for migration, entry and departure, the conditions of work and pay, and the means by which governments can resolve conflicts. It will need also to lay down the codes of government behaviour, to prevent migrants being used as creatures of foreign policy – as when Libya expelled its immigrants as a means of punishing the Arab governments, as Nigeria did its Ghanaians. The political precondition for all this must be a clear assurance to the indigenous population that its own conditions of life – in work and wages, housing, schools and medical services – will not be sacrificed to globalisation.

6 — The Right to Work, the Freedom to Move and the Eradication of World Poverty

> Migration is the oldest action against poverty. It selects those who most want help. It is good for the country to which they go; it helps to break the equilibrium of poverty in the country from which they come. What is the perversity in the human soul that causes people to resist so obvious a good?
>
> J.K. Galbraith

This book has been about the right to work, a right which can only be enjoyed by moving, by migrating between countries. All the world today is supposed to believe in the eradication of poverty, and poverty relates closely to the right to work and so to the freedom to move to where there are jobs. Insofar as the world refuses to allow people to move freely, it chains people in poverty. This is true internationally and domestically. For example, in China there used to be elaborate and tight controls on people's freedom to move around the country. When the World Bank made its first report on China in the early 1980s, it attacked these controls as locking people into poverty, not allowing them to escape. In exactly the same sense, immigration controls in North America, Europe and Japan lock poverty into the developing countries.

Most people do not want to leave their homes, and make no attempt to do so – even when it might seem to outsiders that the conditions of life are intolerably harsh. All the statistical games with differences in per capita incomes, which supposedly show that poverty forces people to move, are defied by this brute reality. Whatever outsiders think, it is always only a tiny minority who can even temporarily face exile, and have the energy, initiative and courage to achieve it. Some may like the adventure, value the experience, but few want to do it other than temporarily – most dream of the day of their return, money in their pocket, to the admiration of their neighbours, relatives and peers. Leaving home is for most people painful, costly and hazardous. For some it is a profoundly alienating experience from which they do not recover. Even those who prosper often weep long afterwards for the land they have lost. This is likely to be especially so for the poorer unskilled worker, the illegal migrant, for whom the barriers and dangers have been specially constructed to frighten and deter, against whom the climate of opinion seems so universally hostile and sometimes physically endangering. It is understandable, there-fore, that such a small proportion of the world's people move. The myth that millions, bags packed, only await the opportunity of a lowering of the guard of developed countries to invade is a fantasy designed to panic people and defraud them, to win their vote or support.

Those who do move usually intend to go only for a short time, for training, experience or to earn a target sum with which to top up family income, build a house, buy equipment or a car, marry or put a child through school. Few hate their home so much, or love so deeply the foreign country in which they work, that they would willingly accept exile. The prototype is the Mexican agricultural worker who runs the awful gauntlet of the US border to work for a season. If the world were without movement controls, the cheapness and speed of air travel make it increasingly possible now to go and return swiftly. But the more numerous the obstacles put in the way of this fast circulation, the greater the incentive to stay longer and, finally and sadly, to accept exile. Immigration regulations oblige people to settle, to 'immigrate', if they are to defend their access to work.

What is at stake in immigration controls is a denial of the right to work. The worker is willing, the work needs to be done (and often creates additional work for the natives), and benefits both the country the migrant enters and the family and country which he or she has left. The tighter the immigration controls, the more the right to work involves illegal migration. Despite the intensification of controls and the growing risks and dangers to the migrant, there is no evidence, while the demand for workers remains so strong, that illegal migration can be ended at a politically tolerable cost. It can only be made more costly and dangerous. As we noted earlier, the immense efforts of the US government to stop the traffic in narcotics, have had no detectable effect on the supply or price of drugs in the US. Unlike narcotics, the US economically benefits from illegal immigration – so if it were stopped, it would damage the livelihood of Americans.

Why can illegal migration not be stopped? After all, it was virtually eliminated in the old Eastern Bloc countries – the Soviet Union and its allies in Eastern Europe and Asia. The question answers itself. Ending illegal migration requires the almost complete closure of a country, turning it into a fortress or a prison. It requires an authoritarian control of the population, with detailed regulation, and a regime of terror. Today, North Korea is one of the few left exercising that kind of control – and the result is an impoverished population, periodically assaulted by famine. Even then it has not completely eliminated the flight of victims of hunger into China. By contrast, the livelihood of developed countries today depends upon having increasingly open economies with increasing worker numbers and volume of movement of each country. Controls on this flow cut at the economic jugular.

It would still be possible to reduce illegal immigration if there were no demand for unskilled workers. As we have seen, the scarcity of such workers has been created and exaggerated by a number of factors – the decline in fertility and the number of years worked, coupled with rising levels of productivity, income and education. The workers who are unemployed are over-qualified to do the low-skill jobs available, and understandably unwilling to submit to such low pay and poor conditions. Could they be automated? Technically, no doubt much could be done if there were no competing imports, so that the cost of automating did not produce goods that were uncompetitive; but that would also require closure and the resulting deterioration in the standard of living of those made redundant. Many of these jobs, in manufacturing, are being relocated abroad. But the mass of jobs are services to the local population that cannot be moved and cannot easily be automated – this is especially true of those in the caring professions who look after the growing number of aged.

Because the economic case against immigration controls is so strong, one must conclude that the real case is not economic at all. People are willing to pay the high costs of controls insofar as they know what they are and can choose. Both the direct costs and the cost of the benefits lost, such as increased employment, are fore-gone for other advantages. They are willing to tolerate the deaths and disablement of many of those trying to cross borders illegally. Immigration, it has been suggested here, is at the heart of a political problem: it supposedly infringes the prerogatives of national sovereignty. The world is in transition from the old economic order of sovereign states, each exercising unchallengeable and absolute power over a territory, a population and a set of economic activities, to one which is to a greater or lesser degree economically integrated. The forms of integration are complicated – from global networks, to chains of interdependent manufacturing and trade, to clusters of activity that span a group of countries. Governments in the new order are obliged to collaborate as a condition of their own economic success and, insofar as they do, relinquish some of the old forms of power over the domestic economy to global markets. The domestic activity within each country becomes a function of markets operating far beyond the territory in which a government exercises power. In the old order, the national interest seemed clear – a government aimed to capture as much activity and wealth within its borders as possible, to stem imports and foreign capital and promote exports and the 'invasion' of foreign markets. Sometimes, governments went even further, and took over major chunks of the economy, at its most extreme in the Soviet Union. The model for competition was warfare, and the difference between 'foreign' and 'native' funda-mental. The state tried to create an economic fortress, as self-sufficient as possible, in order to be invulnerable to the threats of other powers to cut supplies in the event of hostilities. Politically, all this was based – in theory – upon a popular sovereignty rooted in a stable 'homogenous' population, each member endowed with the sup-posedly unique privileges and duties of that nationality.

The old order lasted only a relatively brief time and was only ever partially achieved in most countries. It was at its most extreme in the old Eastern Bloc countries, but elements can be seen in all the great powers, exaggerated by the demands of two world wars and the Great Depression. It was a world in which warfare was seen as a permanent possibility, so that, at the extreme, peace was no more than the interval between wars, the period of preparation to fight. The more realistic planners in government operated on the assumption that society and the economy must be organised to be permanently prepared for war.

The terms for national economic success changed in the long period of boom in the world economy after the Second World War. It became clear that no national economy is big enough to secure the right conditions for growth – in capital, workforce, markets or technology. Each is increasingly dependent upon external trans-actions to secure economic prosperity and growth – or rather the difference between internal and external becomes so blurred that it is steadily more difficult to know where one ends and the other begins. Despite the best efforts of governments to keep the world economy trapped within national concepts, nationality leaks away from both capital and commodities. People still speak of 'Japanese cars' or 'German finance', but integration in manufacturing and capital makes it very difficult to say what the adjective means any longer. (These are large issues which cannot be explored here. Much more detail is contained in my *Of Bread and Guns* [1983], *The End of the Third World* [1987] and *The New Untouchables* [1995]). It becomes increasingly difficult for governments to say what in economic terms is the national interest. Old conditioned reflexes become disastrous. What used to be the pursuit of the national interest now turns out to be damaging to the welfare of citizens – keeping immigrants out does not protect the jobs of the natives, it destroys them.

The change from one order to the other is far from accomplished. National governments remain decisive forces in the world economy, controlling all the institutions which supervise global economic activity. But the trend of integration is by now so well established it seems impossible to reverse – or at least the costs of reversal seem so high it is almost impossible that any government would normally be willing to risk them. If the trend towards integration continues, then national governments become more like local governments, managing fragments of a system of flows which start and end far beyond their knowledge, let alone their power. The old idea of sovereignty will then have gone.

The control of migration is the last great bastion of the old order of national sovereignty, or national protectionism. Indeed, it is in precisely the period in which world economic integration has accelerated that the great powers have made growing efforts to block the logic of integration of workers, to dam the flows, creating closed national pools of labour. As in all fields, the more elaborate the legal regime of regulation, the larger the black economy, of clan-destine operation, designed to defeat the regime. It is almost as if, while governments conspire to undermine their own sovereignty in the economic field as the condition of prosperity (and so political survival), they divert and tolerate the popular xenophobia on which the old regime depended, hostility to migrants being one sector in which they maintain controls. The irrationality is palpable – as in the bizarre collision of sovereignty and labour demand in Hong Kong, (see Appendix III).

In the Hong Kong case, the defence of the old idea of sovereignty took priority not only over compassion for those in flight from persecution and the obligations governments supposedly have to protect those seeking asylum, but also over brute common-sense and the need for workers in the Hong Kong economy. The same irra-tionality governs the refusal of the British and other governments to allow those seeking asylum to work, while complaining bitterly at the cost to public funds of enforcing idleness upon them. Only the desperate delays in processing applications in the UK led to the concession that asylum applicants might work after six months' wait. But in the late summer of 2000, the government reconsidered its stance because the concession, according to the minister concerned, acted 'as a pull factor for applicants who wished to find work in this country but do not qualify for asylum'. This was only one of many measures designed to make the condition for asylum-seekers as miserable as possible, so that illegal immigrants would not try to pass themselves off as refugees. Thus the obligations of compassion were wrecked by the terror of people who wanted to work.

The debate concerning immigration controls has been the most powerful incitement to xenophobia and racism. It has focussed popular hostility (at least in the world of the popular newspapers) on illegal immigrants, and by extension, the cruellest cut of all, on asylum-seekers. As argued in Chapter 3, governments have justified their policies with the opposing argument: the tighter the controls, the fewer people are tempted by racism. European Commission president Romano Prodi repeated the argument early in 2000: tighter border controls were needed to combat the rising tide of xenophobia in Europe. But this is absurdly naïve. On the contrary, the tighter the controls, the more any suspected infringement encourages the most ferocious reaction, prompting a sharp rise in racist attacks, as seen in the flourishing of xenophobia around the issue of asylum-seekers, a campaign orchestrated by governments themselves. With such a degree of misinformation, taxpayers are induced to pay for the pretensions of government – in terms of jobs lost, goods and services not created, let alone the US$8 billion said on one estimate to be the cost of immigration controls in Europe.

Indeed it is even more absurd than that. The ill-paid and foul jobs that migrants are seeking to do are turned by political alchemy into a special privilege, even though native citizens entirely refuse to do them. The right to work in awful jobs is something to be greedy about. It is not inevitable that this need be so. For hundreds of years, workers have been migrating to work across what are supposed to be national frontiers, without any desire to accept exile. Only the nationalist fantasies of the twentieth century induce governments to make it illegal. As we noted earlier, the German *gastarbeiter* system did separate citizenship and work; it failed not because migrants acquired a new desire to become Germans, but because immigration controls made it necessary to settle in order to retain the access to work. But the principle of separating the right to work from the right to settle is not a bad one.

The arrangements agreed within a country to allow newcomers to become citizens are going to vary according to local custom and practice. In some cases, this will no doubt be much more difficult than in others. The arrangements need not affect the right to work. Allowing people to enter a country in order to work is a much smaller order of issue. The benefit is to the country. People need to be aware of the costs of refusing entry both in terms of lost opportunities: a stunted economy, services and goods not being produced and having to be imported at a higher cost; existing citizens being laid off or being paid less; shortages in social facilities and so on. At the moment, such arguments are not presented, and so choices are not made on any sensible basis. Xenophobia, the old gut reaction of hating people for no more sensible reason than that they are foreigners, fills the gap.

If the right to work does not require the need to become a citizen, people should be allowed to come and go as the need for workers changes. Easing this movement of workers helps the economy to grow and improves the livelihood of natives. But what happens during a slump? Migration is determined by the availability of work. If there is no work, workers historically return to their homes, fleeing rising unemployment. The German and French governments tried to enforce that return movement in past recessions, but with limited success, since foreign workers needed to hang on to their right of residence as the condition of getting back to work when the recession was over. Controls ended the historic movement home. Furthermore, many had paid their state insurance contributions and taxes, and expected to receive, in return, unemployment benefits to help them wait out the recession. However, in most countries, state insurance was not insurance at all, but a kind of tax – and benefits were not actuarially related to contributions. In those days, it seemed the state made an open-ended commitment to support almost indefinitely those who were unemployed, and this was unquestioned as a privilege of citizenship. This is now far from the practice of most governments. Reforms and privatisation have narrowed open-ended commitments and brought what you receive much closer to what you pay. Leaving aside what citizens might reasonably expect from their government, temporary foreign workers should get what they paid for as a means to protect the right to work. Unemployed foreign workers should receive the contributions they have made until they are exhausted, either – as some governments have done – in a lump sum or as regular payments in the country of origin or in the country of work. The difference between citizens and foreign workers remains distinct until the second is able to meet whatever criteria is needed to become a citizen. The distinction has to be kept in order to protect the right of migrant workers to enter the country to work without automatically becoming citizens.

If workers can freely migrate to work, there can be no 'illegal' migrants. Apart from giving people access to work, this has several particular advantages. It undercuts the criminal gangs that at present organise the smuggling of workers. They can no longer extract the high prices for smuggling as a result of controls. It also eliminates the appalling slaughter on the borders of those trying to gain entry illegally. The police would then be free to target the much smaller but much worse problem of trafficking in people, especially women and children. Furthermore, once illegal workers become legal, it becomes possible to expose and seek to regulate their working conditions and pay. The workers themselves would then have the right to complain to the authorities without the risk of deportation.

However, all this is not true of refugees. They are driven by fear of their lives, and when countries collapse, there are civil wars or mass persecutions, very large numbers of people can be driven to flight, driven to face extraordinary dangers. It is a cheap fraud that in these circumstances, because they are large in number, their case is dismissed and they are accused of being illegal immigrants, in order to wriggle out of the obligation to protect them. Ending the concept of illegal immigrant blocks up this escape from compassion. If all immigration is legal, the incentive to pretend to be an asylum-seeker ends.

It could then be taken for granted without a great deal of detailed enquiry that in conditions of large-scale social crisis, if thousands of people flee they are genuinely in fear of their lives. Otherwise they would never contemplate such a high-risk strategy, abandoning homes, farms, ways of life. In the long-drawn-out agony of the Balkans, the innocent were driven out. Their treatment in Western Europe is shameful. However, remedies are not easy, since they require international collaboration. At the moment, governments seem only intent on escaping responsibility and offloading the burden onto other countries. Collaboration is equally required to re-establish order in the country in crisis, and this is notoriously difficult. If the crisis is short-lived, the flight is almost invariably temporary and people are anxious to return to their homes. But in other crises, people cannot return. The Russian Jewish flight of the 1890s was only arrested in the Americas; Spanish Republicans and Palestinians are still scattered around the world at large; the

German Jewish expulsions were permanent; some Rwandans have returned home, but not all of them; the people of the Balkans are still in transition.

Mass migrations of this kind are difficult to cope with and demand the kind of government co-operation which ensures an equitable burden on all, so that refugees are treated with compassion. Detention for all – now proposed by the opposition party in Britain – is an outrage in these conditions, punishing refugees for being persecuted and for fleeing. Refugees ought to have the right to work as soon as they arrive, and they would acquire that right if there were free migration for work for everyone. That would relieve the burden on the public exchequer, the supposedly perpetual source of popular rage, or at least focus it upon those in need who cannot easily work – the aged, disabled, single mothers and so on. Removing the accusation of being an illegal immigrant or 'sponging off the welfare services' would help to restore refugees to leading normal lives in their country of refuge until they are able to return, or move on to other destinations, or apply to settle where they are. Since many of the refugees are among the better-educated, they can make an important contribution to meeting the supposed scarcities in the developed countries today. In a sensible world, their talents would be in demand rather than being rejected as if they carried the plague.

A world without migration controls, except such as are required to detect criminal operations, is one in which people are trusted to take sensible decisions, as before the introduction of immigration controls in the twentieth century. Good information about work is crucial to that. What is impressive in international migration is not blind flows, a mass of lemmings leaping into the unknown, but the accuracy and speed with which news of jobs reaches potential workers. The weaknesses of the system are not in people's decisions, but in the failure to facilitate movement and to protect those that move. We still have a world order in which measures of protection exist only for the citizens of a country within that country. Those that fall between countries are treated frequently as without rights, having no legitimate claims on rights, no defences. One of the symbols of this is that we lack an international forum to establish a common order for the movement of people, whether workers or refugees. We have such a forum for trade – GATT, now the WTO – and numerous other regulatory bodies for different sectors of the world economy. But there is no General Agreement on Migration and Refugee Movement that can produce codified rules on how those who move should be treated, the rights and privileges to which people are entitled even when they are outside their own country: the rights of workers in leaving and entering countries, in work, hours, conditions, pay, the standardisation of tax regimes, rules for the transmission of remittances, the transfer of assets, pension and social security savings and so on. Such a forum might also be the place to reprimand governments seeking to use foreign workers as scapegoats in foreign policy disputes. The UN's International Labour Office already combines some of these functions, but there is a case for a more powerful organisation to move governments towards a world of free movement.

We have noted that political leaders are usually the main source of xenophobia, even when they simultaneously denounce it as obnoxious. The reasons are not obscure. Xenophobia is that spontaneous expression of an uncritical loyalty to the status quo which for more than two centuries has been the foundation of nationalism and loyalty to the state. The citizens are more complicated and contradictory than this, and surges of generosity towards, for example, refugees are as common, even if not reported, as instances of hostility. A mild xenophobia is widespread, but this does not necessarily lead to overt racism, let alone physical clashes, except in certain rare circumstances. That needs political leadership. We have seen the shift in the positions of the American, British and French trade unions. Furthermore, with a settled population of immigrant origin, politics change – politicians need to campaign for this vote, and in doing so cannot easily play the xenophobic card. These are straws in the wind and receive little publicity in comparison to a neo-Nazi incident. Yet they offer hope that many people, perhaps even a majority, are much better prepared for a world of global interactions than their governments. Their identities are much less fragile than those who speak of 'cultural invasions' and 'swamping' allow. Indeed, it is precisely in the affirmation of differences that identity is expressed – without this being any necessary cause for conflict.

The regime of immigration control has begun to crumble, so far only by means of yet another affirmation of national egotism – the scramble to get the people with advanced skills from poorer countries, to carry them off, as it were, as imperial booty. In fact, it will not work in this way any longer. Global partnerships in joint operations – programmers staying at home while working for global companies to speed the development of more than one country – will supersede national egotism. But whatever the motives, the sudden reversal on recruiting skilled workers reveals chinks in the heavy armour of national sovereignty. Behind this short-term need looms the problem of ageing and a growing shortage of unskilled labour, the prelude not to each country seeking to steal each others' workers but to sharing technology through global networks, to superseding countries in the reintegration of the world.

That in turn opens up a different world agenda for the eradication of poverty. The existing agenda for tackling poverty covers only half the issues – the freeing of trade through the opening of developed countries' markets, the redistribution of income within and between countries, the creation of programmes of employment and social support for the poor and so on. The other half of the agenda is opening the labour markets of the developed countries to the world's workers. In the relationships between the developed North and the developing South, the biggest failure has not been the decline in aid programmes, which are trivial in the sum of things, or the failure to open markets quickly enough, or transfer technology, but in consistently denying the right to work to the willing and eager workers of the developing countries. In doing this, the developed countries have reduced the prosperity both of their own people and the Third World. Now with the shrinking number of workers in developed countries and the continuing growth in the number of workers in developing countries, the notion of keeping workers and work apart becomes insupportable.

Whether we start from the problem of securing a decent livelihood for the growing number of elderly people in North America, Europe and Japan, or from the problem of how to reduce world poverty, we are led back to how to release the full power of the world's workers. The national enclaves, the demands of sovereignty, block that liberation and enforce a regime that makes poverty inevitable and immovable. The integration of the world economy offers the promise of a solution. But it requires increased movement

– of people, goods, finance, information and ideas. Through the long dark night of the domination of the nation-state, punctuated by the highest achievement of sovereignty, two world wars, that possibility has been sacrificed to the maintenance of national power. Now governments, most of them unwillingly, are being nudged along the way of accepting a decline in sovereignty and thus facilitating movement and the generation of incomes which protect those who do not move. It is a return to a principle of nineteenth century liberalism, sadly lost in the twentieth century of warring states. In the words of the International Emigration Conference in London of 1889:

> We affirm the right of the individual to the fundamental liberty accorded to him [or her] by every civilised nation to come and go and to dispose of his person or his destinies as he pleases.

Appendix I —
Inventing Xenophobia: A British Cautionary Tale

In the mid- to late 1990s, there was an increase in the numbers of people seeking asylum in much of Europe. There were terrible wars and conflicts in the Horn of Africa, the Balkans, Afghanistan and Sri Lanka, and the collapse of order in Iraq, the Congo, Algeria, Colombia and elsewhere, producing the familiar flight of those in terror. Only a tiny proportion of those fleeing left their countries, fewer still got to Europe, and even fewer to Britain. Yet out of this manageable problem, British political leaders invented a catastrophe. It was a re-run of the crisis of the Vietnamese boat people when the rights of refugees were, in the main, blankly denied (see Appendix III). But in this case, the government was covering up a major administrative blunder. The refugees were forced to pay the price.

The government used a procedure to 'fast-track' selected applications for refugee status. People from countries where there was a notorious tyranny, a civil war or other social collapse were to be allowed into Britain with relatively little trouble – without obliging them to prove they were fleeing a real threat to their lives. The government issued lists of such countries from time to time, or rejected applications for countries to be added to the list. But there were delays as the British authorities made up their minds. For example, a 1996 Appeals Tribunal found that the risk to a Kosovan Albanian from Serbian persecution was sufficient to mean that British immigration authorities ought to accept that any people reaching Britain were genuine refugees, and not to repatriate them. The Home Office did not agree, and insisted that Kosovans (like Afghans and Congolese at that time) join the queue for individual examination. As a result, applications dating from 1994 were still awaiting decision in the spring of 1999. Algeria was not accepted until 1998, Somalia 1999 (long after the civil war had quietened down). Home Office delays – compounded by the use of out-of-date or downright misleading information – was one factor in the great pile-up of applications and the delays.

There was a worse fault. A consultancy report to the Home Office in July 1999 – not made public until April 2000 – found that the administration of the Immigration Department was so bad that it could not have handled the flow of applications even if it had been granted the cash and staff it needed. The report showed that the Home Office accepted 19 countries for fast-track applications, but immigration officers at Heathrow airport and at Dover port (between them handling 80 per cent of refugee arrivals) accepted only four (Afghanistan, Liberia, Somalia and the states of the former Yugoslavia) for fast processing. As a result, masses of people who would have been accepted by the Home Office were just put in the queue to wait for a detailed examination. The average delay in decisions, 11 months in July 1999, affecting 77,000 applicants, reached 12 months by April 2000, affecting 100,000.

It seems beyond belief that such a gross bureaucratic error could have occurred and lasted so long – and with such appalling results in terms of the cruelty inflicted on those fleeing torture or the threat of death. Yet it was only the tip of the iceberg. The immigration department compounded the problems by introducing a new procedure (the 'integrated casework system'), new computers and software, and moving premises. In the move, it is said, 9,000 unopened letters were mislaid, thousands of files were made inaccessible by being stored in a car park basement where the fumes kept staff out, passports and documents disappeared, and refugees were obliged to queue for days to be seen. As a result, procedures became sloppier, the treatment of refugees increasingly careless – with the consequence that the number of appeals grew. It is little wonder that critics saw this combination of administrative blunders as a sinister conspiracy to defeat the spirit of the law and reject as many applicants as possible. When, in the spring of 2000, the government set two months as a target for decision-making on applications (with four months to complete the appeals procedure), the staff flatly declared it was impossible, and the staff union called it 'wholly unrealistic'.

Why was it necessary to process applications with such labour? Because British policy was to forbid asylum-seekers to work until they were accepted legally as refugees (with the accumulation of cases and delays leading to an escalation of costs, the government was forced to concede that applicants could work after six months). Since few had any means, they had to be supported by the government while their applications were considered. So with public cash at stake, the examination had to be sufficient to establish that there was a reasonable case. With such an incompetent administration, a small increase could – and did – lead to breakdown. To relieve the cost, applicants were allowed to work. But then they disappeared; they no longer had any reason to be dependent on the government. And if delays in reaching a final decision increased to four or five or six years, families with children in school for that time could hardly be expelled.

The fast-track process – accepting people from particular countries with the minimum of fuss – even if it had worked, was a flawed method of treating refugees. Given that most governments at some stage persecute some of their people, the right to refugee status ought to be accessible to everyone. Furthermore, countries not known as tyrannies, or having wars, also produce people fleeing terror – as with Turkey and its persecution of the Kurds, or Colombia and Algeria. Some countries just could not, according to the Minister, produce refugees – India was an example, and much of Sub-Saharan Africa or Eastern Europe. In the intermediate cases, if the applicant got the chance, he or she had to prove they had been persecuted, which was often almost impossible. Even with medically confirmed evidence of torture, the Minister's heart was not softened – if you had the misfortune to come from North Cyprus. And if in 1997 you came from China – a country which had signed the UN Covenant on Economic, Social and Cultural Rights – you could not possibly have been persecuted.

Administrative errors are always possible, even a run of them of this spectacular kind. But to blame the victims for this is another matter, to seek to punish them so that they will not dare even to arrive is a higher order of governmental criminality. As the administrative machine broke down, increasingly governments began to say the applicants were 'self-evidently' (the word was hardly off the

Minister's lips) bogus, people trying to get on to welfare benefits. UNHCR guidelines urge governments to give asylum-seekers the benefit of the doubt, not only because when you are fleeing for your life you cannot collect the required documents to prove your condition, but also because the results of making a mistake – forcing someone to return to their country – could be so disastrous. Yet in many cases, this is exactly what the government did.

The government and the opposition now began an auction to see who could be more vicious towards the 'self-evidently bogus' 'welfare spongers'. It needed a Monty Python approach to present policies to ensure compassionate treatment of the victims through being increasingly 'tough'. Relentlessly, the opposition attacked the government for being 'soft' (if true, they meant compassionate). The Minister himself was at great pains to prove that he was equally nasty. In a letter to the *Daily Telegraph* (21 January 1999), he rejected with indignation the wicked charge that Britain had the 'most generous asylum laws' in Europe. He boasted that Britain was as low as eleventh among European countries in the number of refugees accepted (relative to the population and GNP). Neither he nor the opposition boasted at how much more they had done for those fleeing terror. On the contrary, the government's response was a new White Paper (with the mocking title, 'Fairer, Faster, Firmer') and a bill to make conditions for asylum-seekers increasingly hard, supposedly to deter them from fleeing for their lives: better stay at home with the enemy you know than face the British you don't.

The contest between government and opposition as to who could be most hostile towards refugees now summoned up another participant, the tabloid press. By 1998, the press launched a collective manhunt in full pursuit of the sinister foreign invader pretending to be a victim. The *Daily Mail* promised that 200,000 of them were poised to launch their assault across the Channel. Indeed, the *Guardian* (12 April 1999) observed that the *Mail* had wrought a change in the language, turning "'asylum-seeker' into a swear-word, a racist epithet as repugnant as 'nigger' or 'Jew'". Other papers heaped wood on the fire: 'a tidal wave of refugees from Eastern Europe is threatening to overwhelm our country' and exploit 'the welfare capital of Europe', 'free-loading off our already overstretched social security system to enjoy a comfortable state-subsidized existence'; 'Alarm as refugees keep flooding in... for easy economic pickings... in honeypot Britain...'; 'Asylum-seekers who raped girl are jailed for five years'.

It was a potent mix – the kindly charitable British abused and defrauded by foreign criminals – and it provided an opportunity to capture political leadership and sell newspapers. If the government responded to the charge of being soft by introducing more draconian rules, the opposition could always up the bid with proposals for something even worse. The government might expand the numbers of asylum-seekers sent to detention (in detention centres or ordinary prisons), astonishingly without charge, trial, fixed sentence or right of appeal. But the opposition went one better and promised that all who came from non-fast-track countries (or as the Shadow Home Secretary put it, 'those countries where there is no genuine risk of persecution') should be imprisoned, should be treated as if they were criminals. This was not, of course, to secure social justice, let alone deliver on the famous British traditions of compassion, but to impose 'a significant deterrent effect on those thinking of travelling here without a well founded case'. There was a surprising lack of concern with the costs of universal detention from a party, the Conservatives, which made the reduction in public spending and taxation its political mantra. According to the government, imprisoning all asylum-seekers would require 20 new detention centres, raising the total bill, with the other costs, to £1.68 billion.

For the opposition, whatever the government did only illustrated that it was 'a soft touch'. It was amazing, if not risible, that this was so endlessly repeated. When the new bill was passed, according to the Shadow Home Minister, it was 'a clear signal to the rest of the world that Britain is a soft touch' (*Hansard*, 9 November 1999). The new regulations constituted 'a soft touch for the organised asylum racketeers who are flooding our country with bogus asylum-seekers'. In the synthetic self-righteous rage into which government and opposition whipped themselves, the plight of refugees, or real people in flight, entirely disappeared, as did the real cause of the problem, the administrative incompetence of the Home Office over a long period of time.

By now the press was set upon such a silly season that, like a nervous horse frightened by a feather in the wind, the pack took off in panic at the mildest event. Thus, when in February 2000 a domestic flight in Afghanistan was highjacked and finally landed at Stansted airport outside London, the 200 passengers, understandably relieved to be liberated, must have been astonished at the howl of rage from the tabloid newspapers. The dazed and dishevelled became, for the *Sun*, a 'flood of freeloaders' coming to a Britain that had become 'dustbin of the world' and, inevitably, 'a soft touch for every scrounger on the planet'. The lack of quickly available accommodation for the passengers apart from the Hilton hotel caused particular anguish. 'Hi, Jack! Where's the four star hotel?' the Mirror invented. And another, 'Stansted Hilton used to house hostages – at £202 for one night'. Perhaps the press would have been soothed had the arrivals been put in tents in a local field – that they came from a hotter climate to the freezing climate of a Britain in February might have delighted them all the more. So enraged were some people, a woman caller to a BBC Radio 5 phone-in programme was able to demand mass sterilisation of all asylum-seekers, to make sure they would not breed in Britain. It marked a true tradition of British compassion.

Another feather in the wind came that spring. A tabloid found a Romanian Roma woman with a child begging. The rage was incandescent, and transmuted this tiny triviality into 'the mounting menace of gipsy spongers'. The imagination of the sub-editors exploded into fantasy – 'Crooks, dole cheats and illegal immigrants pocket £80 billion a year through the black economy'. The *Sun* despatched a reporter to Romania where, unsurprisingly (and without a trace of humour), he found 'gypsy palaces', 'festooned in marble and gold...dubbed Beverly Hills by the locals', entirely financed 'by an army of beggars and dole cheats' in London. Not to be outdone, the *Evening Standard* discovered, also in Romania, 'the town that lives off London's beggars'.

The politicians had conjured up the furies. Yet still they did not desist. The opposition demanded greater punishments for the refugees. And the government responded in March, again cutting the income allowed to asylum-seekers to well below the national poverty level and doubling the fines on those who carried them across borders (and increasing the maximum jail sentence from 7 to 10 years). It satisfied no one. In the local elections that spring, some

Conservative Party leaflets claimed local taxpayers would have to pay an extra £180 each to finance the housing of asylum-seekers (perhaps because the party intended to imprison them all). The government was no doubt inspired when it also released the rumour that it was considering forcing visitors from Asia to make a deposit of £16,000 (or US$24,000) before being allowed into Britain – again, to deter those who overstayed their visa. The outrage of those voters in Britain with relatives and friends in India and Pakistan, combined with the government's embarrassment when it discovered it needed to make efforts to recruit software programmers from the subcontinent, meant this foolish and vindictive proposal was quietly dropped. The same was true of the equally silly proposal from the opposition that all foreign-born doctors in Britain should take an additional English language test.

The auction between government and opposition as to which could be more harsh towards refugees was too much. UNHCR formally condemned the proposal to imprison all asylum-seekers as contrary to fundamental human rights (Article 9 of the Universal Declaration), and reprimanded the two leading parties for inciting racial prejudice on the issue of asylum in the local elections. A Liberal Democrat referred the leaders to the Commission for Racial Equality for the use of racially inflammatory language in the preparations for the May elections. At almost the same time, the monthly Mori polls reported that only 4 per cent of British voters considered asylum-seeking the most important political issue facing the country.

The story was not yet over. In the late summer, British pressure on Calais, the port in France which most travellers used to cross the Channel, led the city council to try to clear the city of those waiting to travel to Britain, that is, make it impossible for anyone to get to the point of claiming asylum. All were thus assumed automatically to be bogus. The British complained that the work of NGOs in sheltering and feeding refugees was encouraging them to persist in trying to get to Britain. The Calais authorities dutifully passed an ordinance forbidding charities to help refugees. Food distribution to the needy was ended. Temporary shelters were closed, forcing families to sleep in the open and beg for food. In the largest park, a journalist found 'more than 200 people camped in the rain with little or no cover, while others were reported to be hiding in temporary refuges, including second World War shelters'. The majority were Kosovan Albanians. Again, this was an impressive affirmation of the proud traditions of British charity towards those in flight.

The British were in no way unique in the cruel and shabby way in which refugees were treated. Nor were they unique in the self-righteous hypocrisy with which the national political leadership covered this flat rejection of their obligations under international law. Certainly, there was nothing distinctive in the government's exploitation of xenophobia to cover the long-standing and extraordinary administrative incompetence of the Home Office. Competitions in xenophobic cruelty had been set off before, creating a climate of disbelief that made it surprising that anyone could ever acquire refugee status. The case is only worth recording because it shows so vividly that the problem of immigration is not the xenophobia of people at large – that exists, but then so do many prejudices without this determining policy. It is the xenophobia of the politicians, their unwillingness to relinquish this hold on people's loyalty in the interests of their pursuit of power.

The innocent victims of this squalid contest were the refugees upon whom were heaped all the favourite prejudices of the politicians and the population – not least the charge of cheating to obtain welfare benefits. They were simply scapegoats. When the tabloid press, unleashed by politicians, went baying after the victims, few had the courage to risk their own political survival by speaking the truth. It would have been laughable if it were not so cruel. But the climate of disbelief, the manufacturing of lies and fantasies, were not so cruel as what resulted on the ground – a rash of racist assaults and incidents which followed the lead given by press and politicians. The leadership had given its permission, and was it surprising that some of the more zealous citizens insisted on implementing the spirit if not the letter of government and opposition policy. The London Police crime reports between 1997 and 2000 show that 42 per cent of people murdered were from ethnic minorities (which represent a quarter of the city's population).

Appendix II —
American Immigration

American immigration law 1882–1996
From racist exclusion to cloning the
nation to worker recruitment

1882   Chinese Exclusion Act: to prohibit immigration of Chinese and prevent the naturalisation of Chinese already in the US.

1907   Agreement with the Japanese government: Japan to restrict emigration to the US.

1917   Immigration Act: first numerical limit set, and national quotas laid down according to the proportions of the US population drawn from those countries in 1910.

1924   Immigration Act: quotas changed to the proportions of the national origins of the US population of 1890 (before the great expansion of immigration from Southern and Eastern Europe, 1900–14).

1924   Japanese Exclusion Act.

1929   Immigration Act: limited entries from the 'Eastern Hemisphere' (the world except the Americas) to 150,000 per year, quotas based on the US population of 1920.

1943–64 The Braceros programme to admit Mexican farm workers on an annual seasonal basis.

1952   Immigration and Nationality Act: national quotas continued, but included a quota for aliens with skills needed.

1965   Immigration and Nationality Act Amendment: ended national quotas; entries in the main to be 'family reunification' (80 per cent), with some allowance for skills; set quota for immigrants from the 'Western Hemisphere' for the first time, and limit of 20,000 per country from the Eastern.

1976   20,000 per country limit extended to the Western Hemisphere.

1980   Refugee Act: removed refugee admissions from the immigration framework, and established provisions for refugee settlement.

1986   Immigration Reform and Control Act: introduced sanctions on employers hiring illegal immigrants; amnesty for existing long-term illegal immigrants (in the event, 2.7 million included); increased border enforcement.

1990   Immigration Act: raised immigration ceilings; tripled employment-based immigrant visas; created a 'diversity' visa for under-represented nationalities (largely Irish initially); increased visas for priority skills and investors with US$1 million or more.

1996   Illegal Immigrant Reform and Immigrant Responsibility Act: summary deportation procedures for illegal aliens; telephone documentation authentication for employers; sharp reduction of legal immigrants' access to welfare provision for first five years; increased border enforcement.

Who gets into Fortress America?

There are five categories of entry visa for settlement (with the right of naturalisation after five years); there is a maximum number permitted under each heading.

1   For the immediate relatives of US nationals: no theoretical limit (but the annual average for 1995–98 was 283,000).

2   For other family members, 226,000 per year (with a waiting list of between 18 months and 11 years; the longest wait currently is 20 years, 11 months for siblings of US nationals born in the Philippines).

3   Diversity visas: 55,000 per year, for entrants with a low representation in immediate past immigration (Europeans and Africans; chosen by annual lottery for those with high-school diploma or two years' work experience).

4   Refugees and asylum-seekers: 100,000 annually.

5   Workers and their families: 140,000 per year (because of restrictions, a third of the allowed number is not used; in 1995–8, there

were 93,000 – roughly 40,000 for workers, 50,000 for their families; quotas for Chinese, Indians, Mexicans and Filipinos were filled). Worker visa subgroups:

EB-1 (40,000): highly skilled 'priority' workers, (without necessarily a job offer), 22,000 used on average, 1995–8.

EB-2 (80,000): advanced professional degrees with job offer, 15,000 taken on average, 1995–8.

EB-3 (10,000): workers filling known shortages after checks that no US nationals are available (the unskilled limited to 10,000); 47,000 taken up, using 7,000 from EB-2. There is a six-year waiting list for unskilled workers.

EB-4 (10,000): for religious ministers and other specified special workers.

As a result of the difficulties of obtaining worker settlement visas, 'temporary worker' visas have expanded: temporary period, usually only one employer, no right to naturalisation.

H1-B (under 50,000 for much of the 1990s): highly skilled, minimum a degree, for three years employment, renewable once. However, numbers reached 60,000 in 1997, when numbers were capped. But in 1998, the numbers allowed were exhausted in eight months, so in October 1998 the cap was lifted to 115,000 for two years and to 107,500 in 2001, when the cap would return to 65,000. The numbers allowed were exhausted in six months, so pressure – particularly from Silicon Valley employers – was on to raise numbers to 150,000 or 200,000.

H2-A: seasonal farm workers.

H2-B: other low-skilled workers, provided none are available in the US; housing and transport to be provided.

There are also special N visas for the college-educated (with a job offer) from Mexico and Canada, to work one year at a time but with indefinite renewability. There is no cap for Canadians, but for Mexicans, 5,500 per year until 2003.

Under the pressure of applications, Congress considered in 2000 revising the provisions for H1-B, H2-A and H2-B visas, or a new guest-worker programme, or ending the cap on EB-2 or EB-3, or ending the requirement for employers to search for natives before securing a visa.

Appendix III — Destroying the Right to Asylum: The Boatpeople

From 1978, three years after the end of the Vietnam War, a million or so people fled by sea from Vietnam. Most were Vietnamese Chinese from the better-off and educated classes of the old pre-communist South Vietnam regime. If the frail craft were not sunk crossing the sea, there were the additional dangers in the waters off Thailand of pirates, who boarded the boats, slaughtered the men and raped and kidnapped the women for sale into prostitution. The death rate is unknown, but assumed to be high, possibly as high as 30–40,000.

At the 1979 Geneva Conference, the Vietnamese government promised to honour the UN Universal Declaration of Human Rights by allowing all who wished to leave Vietnam to do so freely. In panic, the great powers demanded much tighter exit controls to frustrate this right and stop emigration. Later, the Vietnamese offered to release all political prisoners if the US would take them; the US government accepted a selected 10,000.

In general, the neighbouring countries – Thailand, Malaysia, Indonesia, the Philippines, Hong Kong and China – refused to accept refugees. Malaysia, desperate to prevent any increase in the population of Chinese origin (so threatening the Malay majority) towed any refugee boats trying to land back to sea and abandoned them; those that were able to land were interned until moved on to other countries.

Singapore's Prime Minister, Lee Kuan Yew, refused to allow refugees to land. Ships rescuing people at sea were refused entry to Singapore port without depositing a bond with the government of US$4,665. Lee's moral position was cruelly ingenious: 'We would not only be encouraging those responsible to force even more refugees to flee, but also unwittingly demonstrating that a policy of inhumanity does pay dividends'. Foreign Minister Rajaratnam suggested that forcing the boatpeople to flee was a deliberate attempt to destroy the South-east Asian countries by forcing them into a race war.

The Western countries – with the partial exception of Canada, US and Scandinavia – worked hard sitting on their hands. Many left the decision to save people at sea to passing ship captains, themselves under pressure from shipowners and customers (and the refusal of ports and their home countries to allow entry) not to delay cargo by stopping to rescue.

The British government accepted 10,000 (about one per cent of the estimated total). Those who reached Hong Kong, then a British colony, were interned – an extremely expensive procedure – before being moved on to any other country that would take them. By 1989, about 54,000 remained there. The British government dismissed the claim that the boatpeople were refugees, insisting that they were illegal immigrants, driven by poverty, not persecution, to choose this amazingly dangerous way of leaving their country. Being illegal, they could be expelled by force. At 3.00 a.m. on 1 December 1989, 17 women, eight men and 26 children were forced onto an aircraft in Hong Kong and deported to Hanoi – 'a shaming spectacle', as a *Financial Times* editorial called it.

Absurdly, while all this was going on Hong Kong had a considerable shortage of workers, and unskilled workers were being recruited from abroad. By mid-1989, over 44,000 maids had been brought in, and by the end of the year 60,000 (91 per cent Filipina, the rest Thai). Business pressed for more, saying job vacancies were up to 165,000. The government allowed another 20,000, but at the same time increased the penalties for employers hiring illegal immigrants to three years' imprisonment and a HK$200,000 fine (equivalent then to US$25,500), later raised to HK$1 million.

Could the refugees not have been accepted for asylum and allowed to work? Why did the Hong Kong government insist on defying both common-sense and common humanity, and on shouldering the heavy costs of such a contradiction? Just to enforce the law? To discourage others?

The Hong Kong government was not alone in this absurdity. In 2000, at the height of the hysteria in Britain over 'bogus' asylum-seekers, the head of the UK division of the Pirelli tyre company, Lord Limerick, complained to the Minister for Equality: 'It is a scandal that Britain is suffering a skills crisis, while hundreds of highly qualified refugees are being refused the right to work in this country while their cases are being assessed. It's a terrible situation.'

Appendix IV — The Ultimate in Government Foolishness: Singapore

In the 1960s and 1970s, Singapore's government operated strict population control to prevent growth, laying down that couples should have no more than two children.

With extraordinary economic growth, immigrants were drawn in. The government accepted educated and professional immigrants on virtually unlimited 'employment vouchers', but tried to limit strictly all other workers (on 'work permits').

Measures to control ordinary immigrants were draconian – they were not allowed to change jobs for the first three years or hold trade-union office, and protests were liable to lead to deportation. Women immigrants were subject to six-monthly pregnancy tests and not allowed to marry Singapore nationals, except with government permission. If this was granted, couples were required to accept compulsory sterilisation after the second child (this did not affect holders of employment vouchers). If the rule was flouted, immigrants were to be deported, and their Singapore spouses lost the right to cheap public housing, free education for their children and subsidised medical treatment.

In the late 1970s, poor productivity growth in the city was blamed on the availability of unskilled immigrant workers. So this had to be eliminated by making it too expensive. Instead of the former policy of holding down wages, labour costs were now to be increased by 20 per cent per year for three or four years, to force companies to upgrade their efficiency or leave the island. Work permits were cut, and efforts made to cut the immigrant labourforce (for example, in construction), with the aim of eliminating immigrants by 1991, except in domestic, construction and shipyard work.

However, a severe economic contraction in 1985 was blamed in part on high labour costs in the city (increasing 10 per cent per year,

1979–84, while productivity grew at 4.5 per cent annually), or well ahead of the city's nearest rivals. The policy of increasing labour costs was stopped with a wage freeze – but still 60,000 immigrant workers were deported.

The 1981 Singapore census suggested that a third of the city's graduate women failed to marry – as the then Prime Minister Lee Kuan Yew put it, 'the better educated and more rational are not replacing themselves' and 'a multiple replacement rate at the bottom [leads to] a gradual lowering of the general quality of the population'. The government sponsored dating agencies, weekend trips for unmarried graduate couples, procreation tax incentives. However, there were still severe restrictions on the immigration of household help for working mothers, making it impossible for some women to work. Wong Siew Hoon would have been delighted to have a third child while staying at work, but the government fell upon her children's nurse of many years' standing and expelled her. Wong Siew Hoon gave up the idea of another child, since government rules meant that to hire a legal domestic would have taken half her salary (*Los Angeles Times*, 14 May 1989). By contrast, low-skilled women were offered two years' salary to accept sterilisation.

Fears of an ageing population suddenly grew in the 1980s – and so fears of a future decline in population (by 2025, projections suggested that there would be 45 aged 60 or more to every 100 of working age, the ratio worsening if emigration continued). In 1987, a new slogan was introduced: 'At least two. Better three. Four if you can afford it'. A campaign was launched to recruit professionals from abroad (especially from Hong Kong, to join China in 1997).

Unskilled immigrants were still strongly restricted – employers paid a per capita levy to employ them – but with growing shortages of workers, commuters from Malaysia increased (20,000 daily), and in 1988 three-year work permits were allowed for Malaysians. The government urged the elderly and housewives to enter work – without much success.

Efforts continued to punish and expel illegal immigrants, with a S$5,000 (US$2,868) fine or one year's imprisonment for employers (168 were found guilty in 1987); six months' imprisonment and loss of public housing for traffickers. In 1989, after a series of major infrastructure projects, there was a drive to arrest illegal immigrants, have them publicly whipped (three strokes of the cane) and sent to prison for three months.

In August 2000, the government announced a new programme to give parents bonuses of up to S$3,000 (US$1,720) per child if they would have more than one child.

Appendix V —
Average Fees Paid for
Clandestine Travel
and Entry

1 Average from all sources to Europe: US$2–5,000 (Widgren, 1994).
2 Chinese to New York in 1994: US$9–35,000, average US$30,000 (Ko-lin Chin, 1999).
3 Tamils from Sri Lanka to Toronto (1995): CDN$24–26,000 (US$16,139–17,484), 'with good references in Canada' (Canadian Government 1996).
4 Moroccans to Spain by boat (1997): US$600 (EU, 1997); other sources: 500,000 pesetas (£1,850); £1,200.
5 Javanese to Johore, Malaysia (1994): rupiah equivalent of US$110–220, with a rate of interest on advances of 300–500 per cent per annum (Spain, 1994).
6 Albanians to the Italian coast (north of Otranto, Apulia): 1 million lire (US$463).
7 Cyprus to southern Italy (Sicily, Calabria, southern Apulia): 2,500,000 lire (US$1,158).
8 Lithuanians to New York (1997): US$3,750–12,000 (IOM 1997).
9 Calais to Dover, by sea: FF3–4,000 (US$410–547) or £1,500 (UK Home Office) (*Financial Times*, 19–20 August 2000).
10 Rome to Britain (1997): £1,500 (UK Home Office, 1998).
11 Indians to Britain (1997): £6,000–9,000 (UK Home Office, 1998).
12 Chinese to Britain (1997): £16,000 (UK Home Office, 1998).
13 Central Mexico to US (1997): US$2,000.

Appendix VI —
Who Says Silicon Valley is American?

Silicon Valley, California, is the most important global centre of research and development in IT – global in sales, in purchases, in information linkages, and in labourforce.

In 1990, immigrants accounted for at least a third of the scientific and engineering workforce – very much more if you include the children of immigrants. Two-thirds of them were from Asia: 51 per cent from China (including Taiwan), 23 per cent from India, 20 per cent from Vietnam, and the rest from Japan, Korea and the Philippines. Most of them reached the US after 1970, and by 1998, they provided a quarter of the high-tech business of the Valley, generating US$16.8 billion in sales, creating 58,000 jobs.

Chinese and Indian chief executives ran 13 per cent of the Valley's companies, most of them started between 1980 and 1984, 29 per cent of them between 1995 and 1998. Chinese CEOs ran 2,001 companies, with US$13,237 billion sales, employing 41,684 staff. Indian CEOs ran 724 companies, with US$3,588 billion sales, employing 16,598 staff.

But these businesses are part of interdependent global research and development networks which interact with contributing centres in Taiwan, China, India and elsewhere. The staff circulate between these different centres – even the ones who live in the Valley are not 'immigrants', but temporary workers.

Thus, US H-1B visas (see Appendix II) are in fact being used as means not just to enter the US, but to circulate human capital and economic development in IT worldwide.

Source: Saxenian, 1999

A later survey showed that the workforce in the Valley was 49 per cent white, 25 per cent Hispanic, 23 per cent Asian and 3 per cent Afro-American.

Vietnamese Americans employed in IT in the Valley have remitted US$1.2 billion to Vietnam through official channels, and an estimated US$2 billion through unofficial ones since 1996. They have set up 430 companies in Vietnam, with a registered capital of 490 billion dong (US$35 million).

Tables and Figures

Table 1
Foreign or foreign-born population and
labourforce in selected OECD countries
(thousands and percentages)

Foreign population and labourforce

	Foreign population[1]				Foreign labourforce[2]			
	Thousands		% of total population		Thousands		% of total labourforce	
	1987[3]	1997[4]	1987	1997	1987[5]	1997[6]	1987	1997
Austria	326	733	4.3	9.1	158	326	5.4	9.9
Belgium	863	903	8.7	8.9	270	333	6.8	7.9
Denmark	136	250	2.7	4.7	63	88	2.1	3.1
Finland	18	81	0.4	1.6		19		0.8
France	3714	3597	6.8	6.3	1525	1570	6.3	6.1
Germany	4241	7366	6.9	9.0	1866	2522	6.9	9.1
Ireland	77	114	2.2	3.1	33	52	2.5	3.4
Italy	572	1241	1.0	2.2	285	332	1.3	1.7
Japan	884	1483	0.7	1.2		660[7]		1.0
Luxembourg	103	148	26.8	34.9	64[8]	125[8]	37.6	55.1
Netherlands	592	678	4.0	4.4	176	208	3.0	2.9
Norway	124	158	2.9	3.6	49[9]	60[9]	2.3	2.8
Portugal	95	175	1.0	1.8	46	88	1.0	1.8
Spain	335	610	0.9	1.5	58	176	0.4	1.1
Sweden	401	552	4.8	6.0	215	220	4.9	5.2
Switzerland	979	1341	14.9	19.0	588[10]	693[10]	16.6	17.5
UK	1839	2066	3.2	3.6	815	949	3.3	3.6

Foreign population and labourforce

	Foreign population[11]				Foreign labourforce[11]			
	Thousands		% of total population		Thousands		% of total labourforce	
	1986[12]	1996	1986	1996	1986[12]	1996[13]	1986	1996
Australia	3247	3908	20.8	21.1	1901	2239	25.4	24.6
Canada	3908	4971	15.4	17.4	2359	2681	18.5	18.5
US	14080	24600	6.2	9.3	7077	14300	6.7	10.8

Notes on Table 1

1 Data are from population registers except for France (census), Ireland and the United Kingdom (Labour Force Survey), Japan and Switzerland (register of foreigners) and Italy, Portugal and Spain (residence permits).
2 Data include the unemployed except for Italy, Luxembourg, the Netherlands, Norway and the United Kingdom. Data for Austria, Germany and Luxembourg are from Social Security registers, for Denmark and Norway from the register of population and the register of employees respectively. Data for Italy, Portugal, Spain and Switzerland are from residence or work permits. Figures from Japan and the Netherlands are estimates from national Statistical Offices. For other countries data are from Labour Force Surveys.
3 1982 for France; 1988 for Portugal.
4 1990 for France; 1996 for Denmark.
5 1988 for Norway, Portugal and Spain; 1991 for Italy; 1986 for Belgium.
6 1995 for Italy; 1986 for Denmark.
7 Data are estimates and include those of Japanese descent, students and illegal workers.
8 Including cross-border workers.
9 Excluding the self-employed.
10 Number of foreigners with an annual residence permit or a settlement permit who engage in gainful activity. Seasonal and cross-border workers are excluded.
11 Data are from censuses except for the United States in 1996 (estimates from the *Current Population Survey*).
12 1980 for the United States.
13 1991 for Canada

Sources: National Statistical Institutes; Sopemi (1999)

Table 2
Stocks of foreign population in selected OECD countries
(thousands and percentages)

	1988	1989	1990	1991	1992	1993	1994	1995	1996	1997
Austria	344.0	387.2	456.1	532.7	623.0	689.6	713.5	723.5	728.2	732.7
% total pop.	4.5	5.1	5.9	6.8	7.9	8.6	8.9	9.0	9.0	9.1
Belgium	868.8	880.8	904.5	922.5	909.3	920.6	922.3	909.8	911.9	903.2
% total pop.	8.8	8.9	9.1	9.2	9.0	9.1	9.1	9.0	9.0	8.9
Czech Rep.	–	–	–	–	41.2	77.7	103.7	158.6	198.6	209.8
% total pop.	–	–	–	–	0.4	0.8	1.0	1.5	1.9	2.0
Denmark	142.0	150.6	160.6	169.5	180.1	189.0	196.7	222.7	237.7	249.6
% total pop.	2.8	2.9	3.1	3.3	3.5	3.6	3.8	4.2	4.7	4.7
Finland	18.7	21.2	26.3	37.6	46.3	55.6	62.0	68.6	73.8	80.6
% total pop.	0.4	0.4	0.5	0.8	0.9	1.1	1.2	1.3	1.4	1.6
France	–	–	3596.6	–	–	–	–	–	–	–
% total pop.	–	–	6.3	–	–	–	–	–	–	–
Germany	4489.1	4845.9	5342.5	5882.3	6495.8	6878.1	6990.5	7173.9	7314.0	7365.8
% total pop.	7.3	7.7	8.4	7.3	8.0	8.5	8.6	8.8	8.9	9.0
Hungary	–	–	–	–	–	–	137.9	139.9	142.2	143.8
% total pop.	–	–	–	–	–	–	1.3	1.4	1.4	1.4
Ireland	82.0	78.0	80.0	87.7	94.9	89.9	91.1	96.1	118.0	114.4
% total pop.	2.4	2.3	2.3	2.5	2.7	2.7	2.7	2.7	3.2	3.1
Italy	645.4	490.4	781.1	863.0	925.2	987.4	922.7	991.4	1095.6	1240.7
% total pop.	1.1	0.9	1.4	1.5	1.6	1.7	1.6	1.7	2.0	–
Japan	941.0	984.5	1075.3	1218.9	1281.6	1320.7	1354.0	1362.4	1415.1	1482.7
% total pop.	0.8	0.8	0.9	1.0	1.0	1.1	1.1	1.1	1.1	1.2
Korea	45.1	47.2	49.5	51.0	55.8	66.7	84.9	110.0	148.7	176.9
% total pop.	0.1	0.1	0.1	0.1	0.1	0.2	0.2	0.2	0.3	–
Luxembourg	105.8	106.9	113.1	117.8	122.7	127.6	132.5	138.1	142.8	147.7
% total pop.	27.4	27.9	29.4	30.2	31.0	31.8	32.6	33.4	34.1	34.9
Netherlands	623.7	641.9	692.4	732.9	757.4	779.8	757.1	725.4	679.9	678.1
% total pop.	4.2	4.3	4.6	4.8	5.0	5.1	5.0	4.7	4.4	–
Norway	135.9	140.3	143.3	147.8	154.0	162.3	164.0	160.8	157.5	158.0
% total pop.	3.2	3.3	3.4	3.5	3.6	3.8	3.8	3.7	3.6	3.6
Portugal	94.7	101.0	107.8	114.0	123.6	131.6	157.1	168.3	172.9	175.3
% total pop.	1.0	1.0	1.1	1.2	1.3	1.3	1.6	1.7	1.7	1.8
Spain	360.0	249.6	278.7	360.7	393.1	430.4	461.4	499.8	539.0	609.8
% total pop.	0.9	0.6	0.7	0.9	1.0	1.1	1.2	1.2	1.3	1.5
Sweden	421.0	456.0	483.7	493.8	499.1	507.5	537.4	531.8	526.6	522.0
% total pop.	5.0	5.3	5.6	5.7	5.7	5.8	6.1	5.2	6.0	6.0
Switzerland	1006.5	1040.3	1100.3	1163.2	1213.5	1260.3	1300.1	1330.6	1337.6	1340.8
% total pop.	15.2	15.6	16.3	17.1	17.6	18.1	18.6	18.9	18.9	19.0
UK	1821.0	1821.0	1723.0	1750.0	1985.0	2001.0	2032.0	1948.0	1934.0	2066.0
% total pop.	3.2	3.2	3.2	3.1	3.5	3.5	3.6	3.4	3.4	3.6
US	–	–	11,770.3	–	–	–	–	–	–	–
% total pop.	–	–	4.7	–	–	–	–	–	–	–

Note on Table 2
Data are from population registers or from the register of foreigners except for France and the United States (census). Portugal and Spain (residence permits). Ireland and the United Kingdom (Labour Force Survey) and refer to the population on 31 December of the years indicated unless otherwise stated.

Source: Sopemi (1999)

Table 3
United Kingdom, inflows of foreign population by nationality

Thousands

	1992	1993	1994	1995	1996	1997
US	43.9	37.3	38.2	39.4	43.2	42.5
Australia	25.0	21.5	27.2	26.6	25.1	26.5
India	9.2	8.9	9.9	11.6	13.0	16.1
South Africa	2.3	2.6	5.6	11.1	12.9	13.0
New Zealand	10.6	9.3	12.1	12.0	11.0	12.1
Japan	10.4	9.4	10.4	10.1	10.8	10.4
Pakistan	8.3	7.5	6.6	7.2	9.6	7.8
Canada	6.4	5.8	6.7	6.7	7.4	8.3
Philippines	2.6	3.3	5.2	6.5	6.8	7.5
Poland	3.5	3.5	3.5	3.5	3.6	5.4
Korea	–	1.5	2.0	2.5	3.2	4.2
Bangladesh	3.2	3.2	3.2	2.8	3.3	4.0
Russian Federation	–		3.5	4.2	3.6	4.0
Malaysia	3.0	3.0	3.3	3.5	3.3	3.6
China	1.8	2.3	2.7	3.2	3.2	2.5
Other countries	73.6	71.2	53.4	55.6	58.3	67.3
Total	**203.9**	**190.3**	**193.6**	**206.3**	**216.4**	**236.9**

Note on Table 3
Passengers, excluding European Economic Area nationals, admitted to the United Kingdom. Data exclude visitors, passengers in transit or returning on limited leave or who previously settled. Students and au pair girls are excluded.

Source: Sopmei (1999)

Table 4
Stock of Asian nationals[1] in selected OECD countries in 1997
(thousands and percentages)

	Japan[2]		Denmark		France		Germany		Italy		Korea	
	'000	%	'000	%	'000	%	'000	%	'000	%	'000	%
Tot. Foreigners	1482.7	100.0	249.6	100.0	3596.6	100.0	7365.8	100.0	1240.7	100.0	176.9	100.0
Asia[3] of which:	1086.4	73.3	52.3	21.3	227.0	6.3	–	–	225.5	18.2	–	–
Bangladesh	6.1	0.4	–	–	–	–	–	–	–	–	7.9	4.5
China	252.2	17.0	2.1	0.8	14.1	0.4	36.7	0.5	37.8	3.0	35.4	20.0
India	7.5	0.5	1.1	0.4	4.6	0.1	35.6	0.5	22.6	1.8	–	–
Indonesia	11.9	0.8	–	–	1.3	–	–	–	–	–	13.6	7.7
Korea	645.4	43.5	–	–	4.3	0.1	21.9	0.3	–	–	–	–
Pakistan	5.6	0.4	6.9	2.8	9.8	0.3	–	–	–	–	1.7	0.9
Philippines	93.3	6.3	2.1	0.8	1.9	0.1	–	–	61.3	4.9	13.1	7.4
Sri Lanka			5.4	2.2	10.3	0.3	60.3	0.8	28.2	2.3	3.7	2.1
Vietnam	11.9	0.8	5.2	2.1	33.7	0.9	87.9	1.2	–	–	13.5	7.6
Tot. for above 9 countries	1033.8	69.7	22.9	9.2	80.0	2.2	242.5	3.3	149.9	12.1	88.8	50.2

	Netherlands		Norway		Spain		Sweden		Switzerland		UK	
	'000	%	'000	%	'000	%	'000	%	'000	%	'000	%
Tot. Foreigners	678.1	100.0	158.0	100.0	609.8	100.0	522.0	100.0	1243.6	100.0	2066	100.0
Asia[3] of which:	69.0	10.2	31.5	19.9	49.1	8.1	90.3	17.3	–	–	490	23.7
Bangladesh	0.5	0.1	–	–	–	–	1.0	0.2	0.3	–	63	3.0
China	7.3	1.1	1.8	1.2	15.8	2.6	3.7	0.7	3.4	0.3	21	1.0
India	2.8	0.4	2.2	1.4	6.8	1.1	1.7	0.3	4.4	0.4	110	5.3
Indonesia	8.0	1.2					0.4	0.1	0.9	0.1	–	–
Korea	–	–	0.2	0.1	–	–	0.5	0.1	0.8	0.1	–	–
Pakistan	3.2	0.5	7.5	4.7	–	–	0.9	0.2	1.2	0.1	68	3.3
Philippines	2.4	0.4	1.6	1.0	11.4	1.9	2.0	0.4	3.0	0.2	15	0.7
Sri Lanka	2.4	0.4	3.8	2.4	–	–	1.0	0.2	7.0	0.6	26	1.3
Vietnam	2.0	0.3	3.5	2.2	–	–	2.8	0.5	7.4	0.6	–	–
Tot. for above 9 countries	28.5	4.2	20.7	13.1	33.9	5.6	14.1	2.7	28.4	2.3	303	14.7

Notes on Table 4
1   Data are from population registers (or registers of foreigners) except for France (census), Italy and Spain (residence permits) and the United Kingdom (Labour Force Survey). Figures are for 1990 for France, 1992 for Switzerland.
2   Data for China include Chinese Taipei.
3   Including the Middle East.

Sources: National Statistical Institutes; Sopemi (1999)

Table 5
Non-immigrants[1] admitted by class of admission, fiscal years 1994–96, US
(thousands)

	1994	1995	1996
Foreign government officials, spouses and children	105.3	103.6	118.2
Temporary visitors for business	3164.1	3275.3	3770.3
Temporary visitors for pleasure	17,154.8	17,611.5	19,109.9
Transit Aliens	330.9	320.3	325.5
Students	386.2	356.6	418.1
Vocational students	7.8	7.6	8.8
Spouses and children of students	33.7	31.3	32.5
International representatives, spouses and children	74.4	72.0	79.5
Temporary workers	450.0	464.6	533.5
Registered nurses	6.1	6.5	2.0
Professionals	105.9	117.6	144.5
Temporary agricultural workers	13.2	11.4	9.6
Temporary non-agricultural workers	15.7	14.2	14.3
Industrial trainees	3.1	2.8	3.0
Professional workers: North American Free Trade Agreement	24.8	23.9	27.0
Workers with extraordinary ability	5.0	6.0	7.2
Workers accompanying the workers with extraordinary ability	1.5	1.8	2.1
Athletes and entertainers	28.1	28.4	33.6
International cultural exchange	1.5	1.4	2.1
Workers in non-profit religious organisations	6.0	6.7	9.0
Intra-company transferees	98.2	112.1	140.5
Treaty traders and investors and dependents	141.0	131.8	138.6
Spouses and children of temporary workers[2]	43.2	46.4	53.6
Spouses and children of NAFTA professionals	6.0	7.2	7.7
Spouses and children of intra-company transferees	56.0	61.6	73.3
Representatives of foreign information media and dependents	27.7	24.2	33.6
Exchange visitors	216.6	201.1	215.5
Spouses and children of exchange visitors	42.6	39.3	41.3
Fiancé(es) of US citizens	8.1	7.8	9.0
Children of fiancé(es)	0.8	7.8	1.0
NATO, officials their spouses and children	9.1	8.6	10.9
Unknown	0.9	0.8	0.3
Total	**22,118.7**	**22,640.5**	**24,842.5**

Notes on Table 5

1   Non-immigrants are visitors, persons in transit or persons granted temporary residence permits. Data may be over estimated as they include multiple entries by the same person over time.

2   Excluding spouses and children of NAFTA professionals and intra-company transferees.

Sources: US Department of Justice, *1996 Statistical Yearbook of the Immigration and Naturalisation Service*; Sopemi (1999)

Table 6
Entries of temporary workers in certain OECD countries by principal categories, 1992, 1996–97
(thousands)

	1992	1996	1997
Australia			
Skilled temporary resident programme[1]	14.6	15.4	12.5
Working holiday makers	25.9	40.3	50.0
Total	**40.5**	**55.7**	**62.5**
	(40.5)	*(20.0)*	*(19.7)*
Canada[2]			
Highly skilled workers			
Workers whose employment requires approval[3]	66.4	–	–
Professionals[4]	5.3	–	–
Reciprocal employment[4, 5]	5.6	–	–
Workers with significant benefits to Canada[4]	4.6	–	–
Seasonal workers	11.1	–	–
Total	**92.9**	–	–
	(230.4)	–	–
France			
Highly skilled workers			
Employees on secondment[6]	0.9	0.8	1.0
Researchers[6]	0.9	1.2	1.1
Seasonal workers	13.6	8.8	8.2
Total	**15.4**	**10.8**	**10.3**
	(42.3)	*(11.5)*	*(11.0)*
Germany			
Workers employed under contract for services	115.1	47.3	42.1
Seasonal workers	212.4	220.9	226.0
Trainees	5.1	4.3	3.2
Total	**332.6**	**272.5**	**271.2**
	(408.9)	*(262.5)*	*(285.4)*
Japan			
Highly skilled workers	108.1	78.5	93.9
Korea			
Highly skilled workers	–	36.7	42.2
Trainees	9.7	53.2	51.1
Total	–	**90.0**	**93.3**
Switzerland			
Seasonal workers	126.1	62.7	46.7
Trainees	1.6	0.7	0.7
Total	**127.8**	**63.4**	**47.4**
	(39.7)	*(24.5)*	*(25.4)*
UK			
Highly skilled workers (long term permits)[7]	12.7	16.9	18.7
Short term permit holders	14.0	16.8	19.0
Working holiday-makers	24.0	33.0	33.3
Trainees	3.4	4.0	4.7
Total	**54.1**	**70.7**	**75.7**
US[8]			
Highly skilled workers			
Specialists (visa H-B1)	110.2	144.5	
Specialists (NAFTA, visa TN)[9]	12.5	27.0	
Workers of distinguished abilities (Visa O)	0.5	7.2	
Seasonal workers (visa H-2A)	16.4	9.6	
Industrial (visa H-3)	3.4	3.0	
Total	**143.0**	**191.2**	
	(116.2)	*(117.5)*	*(90.6)*

Notes on Table 6

The categories of temporary workers differ from one country to another. Only the principal categories of temporary workers are presented in this table. The figures in brackets indicate the number of entries of permanent workers.

1 The data cover the fiscal year (from July to June of the intended year) and include accompanying persons.
2 The figures are for the number of work permits issued. The data are likely to be over-estimates in as far as one person might obtain multiple entries in one year.
3 The list of eligible jobs excludes unskilled jobs, those restricted to Canadian citizens and those with high rates of unemployment.
4 These workers do not require approval by the Government employment service.
5 This category concerns in particular academics and researchers admitted within the framework of bilateral agreements between certain specialists.
6 Beneficiaries of provisional work permits (APT).
7 Long-term permits (one year and over) are mostly accorded to specialists and senior managers.
8 The data cover the fiscal year (October to September of the indicated year). A person is counted as many times as he enters the country over the course of the same year. The data may well therefore be over-estimates.
9 The figures include family members.

Sources: Australia: Department of Immigration and Ethnic Affairs (DIEA); Canada: Citizenship and Immigration Canada; France: Office des migrations internationales, *Annuaire des migrations 97*; Germany: Budesanstalt fur Arbeit; Japan: Ministry of Justice; Korea: Ministry of Justice; Switzerland: Office Federal des etrangers; United Kingdom: Department of Employment; United States: United States Department of Employment, *1996 Statistical Yearbook of Immigration and Naturalisation Service*; Sopemi (1999)

Table 7
Comparison between the ranking of asylum and refugee nationalities and those nationalities that were most frequently smuggled or trafficked into the EU during 1998

| | Top ten countries of origin for asylum claims in Europe during 1998[1] | Top ten countries in terms of asylum recognition (resulting in either 1951 Convention Status or a humanitarian status in Europe)[2] | Top ten countries of origin of migrants where the method of irregular entry into the EU was the result of trafficking or smuggling activities that have been intercepted by the national authorities during 1998 | | | |
			IGC[3]	UK[4]	Germany[5]	Hungary[6]
1	FR Yug.	Bosnia/Herz.	Iraq	FR Yug.	FR Yug.	FR Yug.
2	Iraq	Iraq	FR Yug.	Sri Lanka	Afghan.	Romania
3	Turkey	FR Yug.	Afghan.	Albania	Romania	Afghan.
4	Afghan.	Turkey	Albania	Romania	Iraq	Bangladesh
5	Sri Lanka	Somalia	Romania	Pakistan	Turkey	Iraq
6	Somalia	Iran	Somalia	India	Macedonia	China
7	Bosnia/Herz.	Sri Lanka	Sri Lanka	China	Sri Lanka	Turkey
8	Romania	Afghan.	Turkey	Nigeria	Vietnam	Sierra L.
9	Iran	Ethiopia	Poland	Poland	China	Algeria
10	Algeria	Vietnam	India	Turkey	Bulgaria	Moldova

Notes on Table 7

1 Derived from UNHCR (1999) Table VI.I Asylum applications by origin, Europe, *Statistical Overview 1998*, UNHCR, Geneva.

2 Derived from UNHCR (1999) figures for 1989-98 op. cit. Table VI.8.

3 Membership of IGC. Communication to the author from the Secretariat of the *International Governmental Consultations (IGC)*, January 2000.

4 The United Kingdom. Communication to the author by the *Immigration and Nationality Department* of the *Home Office*, Croydon, January 2000. Figures relate to all those attempting illegal entry in 1998 – 56 per cent was clandestine. The ranking of illegal entrants that go on to claim asylum is virtually identical, save the promotion of 'Turkey' to 9th position (in place of 'Poland') and the inclusion of 'Algeria' in 10th place.

5 Germany. Derived from figures for smuggling interceptions in 1998 prepared for this report by *Grenzschutzdirektion* in Koblenz, January 2000.

6 Hungary. Figures given to the author by the ICMPD office at the HQ of the Hungarian border police, January 2000.

Source: Morrison (2000)

Table 8
Asylum claims and refugee status determination by EU states relating to nationals from the 'Action Plan' countries during 1998[1,2]

Country of origin	Country of asylum						
	Austria	Belgium	Denmark	Finland	France	Germany	Greece
Afghanistan	316 51 **16.1**	*No* *figures* *given*	360 219 **60.8**	*No* *figures* *given*	*No* *figures* *given*	5716 1948 **34.1**	126 2 **1.6**
FR Yugoslavia (including Kosovo)	3725 124 **3.3**	514 140 **27.2**	387 242 **62.5**	197 93 **47.2**	871 185 **21.2**	41,460 1171 **2.8**	*No* *figures* *given*
Iraq	2020 77 **3.8**	199 51 **25.6**	1732 1511 **87.2**	*No* *figures* *given*	287 134 **46.7**	9720 3641 **37.5**	3470 69 **6.8**
Somalia	*No* *figures* *given*	*No* *figures* *given*	930 857 **92.2**	126 108 **85.7**	*No* *figures* *given*	1175 170 **14.8**	*No* *figures* *given*
Sri Lanka	124 1 **0.8**	*No* *figures* *given*	142 54 **39.4**	*No* *figures* *given*	1583 816 **51.5**	4395 243 **5.5**	*No* *figures* *given*

Country of origin	Country of asylum						
	Ireland	Italy	N/lands	Portugal	Spain	Sweden	UK
Afghanistan	*No* *figures* *given*	*No* *figures* *given*	6927 3,987 **57.6**	*No* *figures* *given*	*No* *figures* *given*	240 168 **70.0**	1605 1535 **95.6**
FR Yugoslavia (including Kosovo)	*No* *figures* *given*	397 101 **25.4**	2734 55 **6.0**	*No* *figures* *given*	*No* *figures* *given*	3237 1,249 **38.6**	1575 1,010 **64.1**
Iraq	*No* *figures* *given*	1232 323 **26.2**	11,851 5987 **50.5**	*No* *figures* *given*	113 32 **31.0**	3090 2329 **75.4**	1095 1,010 **92.2**
Somalia	150 54 **36.0**	*No* *figures* *given*	2425 875 **36.1**	*No* *figures* *given*	*No* *figures* *given*	232 124 **53.4**	2805 2705 **96.4**
Sri Lanka	*No* *figures* *given*	*No* *figures* *given*	1,460 161 **11.0**	*No* *figures* *given*	*No* *figures* *given*	*No* *figures* *given*	2,010 60 **3.0**

Key
Total number of cases decided within 1998.
Total number recognised as refugees (1951 Convention) or gaining humanitarian status.
Total recognition rate (%).

Notes on Table 8
1   There are many other applications in other European states not part of the EU.
2   Derived from UNHCR (1999) op. cit., Table IV.3.

Source: Morrison (2000)

Table 9
Inflows of asylum-seekers into selected OECD countries
(thousands)

	1989	1990	1991	1992	1993	1994	1995	1996	1997	1998
Australia	0.5	3.8	17.0	4.1	4.6	4.2	5.1	6.0	9.3	7.8
Austria	21.9	22.8	27.3	16.2	4.7	5.1	5.9	7.0	6.7	13.8
Belgium	8.2	13.0	15.4	17.6	26.5	14.7	11.7	12.4	11.8	22.0
Canada	19.9	36.7	32.3	37.7	21.1	21.7	25.6	25.7	22.6	22.6
Czech Rep.	–	1.8	2.0	0.9	2.2	1.2	1.4	2.2	2.1	4.1
Denmark	4.6	5.3	4.6	13.9	14.3	6.7	5.1	5.9	5.1	5.7
Finland	0.2	2.7	2.1	3.6	2.0	0.8	0.8	0.7	1.0	1.3
France	61.4	54.8	47.4	28.9	27.6	26.0	20.4	17.4	21.4	21.8
Germany	121.3	193.1	256.1	438.2	322.6	127.2	127.9	116.4	104.4	98.7
Greece	6.5	4.1	2.7	2.0	0.8	1.3	1.4	1.6	4.4	2.6
Hungary	–	–	–	–	–	–	–	–	1.1	7.4
Ireland	–	0.1	–	–	0.1	0.4	0.4	1.2	3.9	4.6
Italy	2.3	4.7	31.7	2.6	1.3	1.8	1.7	0.7	1.9	4.7
Luxembourg	0.1	0.1	0.2	0.1	0.2	0.2	0.2	0.3	0.4	1.6
Netherlands	13.9	21.2	21.6	20.3	35.4	52.6	29.3	22.9	34.4	45.2
Norway	4.4	4.0	4.6	5.2	12.9	3.4	1.5	1.8	2.3	8.3
Poland	–	–	–	–	–	0.6	0.8	3.2	3.5	2.9
Portugal	0.1	0.1	0.2	0.6	2.1	0.8	0.5	0.3	0.3	0.3
Spain	4.1	8.6	8.1	11.7	12.6	12.0	5.7	4.7	5.0	6.5
Sweden	30.0	29.4	27.4	84.0	37.6	18.6	9.0	5.8	9.6	13.0
Switzerland	24.4	35.8	41.6	18.0	24.7	16.1	17.0	18.0	24.0	41.2
UK	16.8	38.2	73.4	32.3	28.0	42.2	55.0	37.0	41.5	57.7
US	101.7	73.6	56.3	104.0	144.2	146.5	154.5	128.2	79.8	50.8

Source: Sopemi (1999)

Table 10
'Youthfulness' indicator[1] by principal regions in 1999
(percentages)

	Proportion aged below 15 years	Proportion aged above 64 years	Youthfulness[1] indicator
Africa	43	3	40
North Africa	38	4	34
West Africa	45	3	42
East Africa	46	3	43
Central Africa	47	3	44
Southern Africa	35	5	30
Asia	32	6	26
Western Asia	37	4	33
Central-southern Asia	37	4	33
South-east Asia	34	4	30
East Asia	25	8	17
of which: China	26	7	19
America	29	8	21
North America	21	13	8
Central America	36	4	32
Caribbean	31	7	24
South America	32	6	26
Oceania	26	10	16
Russian Federation	20	13	7
Europe (not incl. Russian Federation)	18	15	3
Northern Europe	19	15	4
Western Europe	17	15	2
Eastern Europe	20	13	7
Southern Europe	17	16	1
World	31	7	24
OECD	21	13	8
of which:			
Mexico	35	5	30
Turkey	31	5	26
Australia	21	12	9
US	21	13	8
Poland	21	12	9
Canada	20	12	8
France	19	16	3
United Kingdom	19	16	3
Sweden	19	17	2
Germany	16	16	–
Spain	15	16	–1
Italy	15	17	–2
Japan	15	16	-1

Note on Table 10

1   Proportion aged below 15 years (%) minus the proportion aged over 64 years (%).

Sources: Calculations by INED (Institut national d'études démographiques) from Population Reference Bureau data; Sopemi (1999)

Table 11
Remittances for a selection of countries, 1989

	Remittances: US$ billions	As % of export earnings	As % of official aid
Yugoslavia	6.3	47	–
Egypt	4.3	166	270
Portugal	3.4	26	–
Turkey	3.0	26	–
India	2.7	17	141
Pakistan	1.9	41	17
Morocco	1.3	40	299
Bangladesh	0.8	59	43
Jordan	0.6	61	200
Tunisia	0.5	16	195
Colombia	0.5	8	740
Philippines	0.4	5	43

Source: UNDP (1992)

Figure 1
Immigration flows into selected OECD countries
by main categories[1] in 1997
(percentages of total inflows)

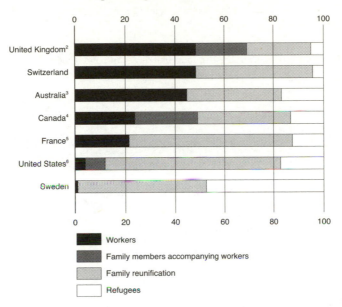

Workers

Family members accompanying workers

Family reunification

Refugees

Notes on Figure 1

Countries are ranked by decreasing order of the percentage of workers in total inflows.

1 For Australia, Canada, the US and Sweden, data concern acceptances for settlement. For Switzerland and France, entries correspond to residence permits delivered in general for a period longer than one year. For the United Kingdom, data are based on entry control at ports of certain categories of migrants (excluding European Economic Area citizens). For Switzerland, France and Sweden, family members accompanying workers are included under 'Family reunification'. For Australia, 'Workers' include accompanying dependents.

2 Passengers, excluding European Economic Area nationals, admitted to the UK. The data only include certain categories of migrants: work permit holders, spouses and refugees (excluding residents returning on limited leave or who previously settled). The category 'Workers' include Commonwealth citizens with a UK-born grandparent who are taking or seeking employment.

3 Data refer to fiscal year (July 1997 to June 1998). Excluding the Special Eligibility programme. The category 'Workers' includes accompanying dependents.

4 Excluding the retired.

5 Inflows of family members of EU citizens are estimated. Excluding visitors and persons who benefited from the regularisation programme.

6 Data refer to fiscal year (October 1996 to September 1997). Excluding immigrants who obtained a permanent residence permit following the 1986 Immigration Reform and Control Act.

Sources: National Statistical Institutes; Sopemi (1999)

Figure 2
Share of mixed marriages[1] in total marriages in some OECD countries, last available year[2]

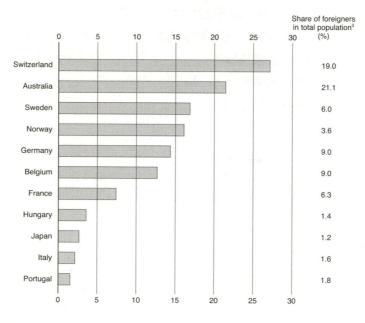

	Share of foreigners in total population[3] (%)
Switzerland	19.0
Australia	21.1
Sweden	6.0
Norway	3.6
Germany	9.0
Belgium	9.0
France	6.3
Hungary	1.4
Japan	1.2
Italy	1.6
Portugal	1.8

Notes on Figure 2
1 A mixed marriage is one between a foreigner and a national of the country in which he/she is residing (in the case of Australia, between a person born abroad and a person born in the country).
2 1997 except for Austria, Belgium, France, Hungary, Sweden (1996), and Italy (1994).
3 1997 except for Austria, Belgium, Hungary, Sweden (1996), France (1990) and Italy (1994). For Australia, proportion of foreign-born in total population.

Sources: Australia: ABS; Belgium: National Statistical Office; France: INSEE; Germany: Statistches Bundesamt; Hungary: Civil registers; Italy: ISTAT; Japan: Ministry of Health; Norway: Statistics Norway; Portugal: National Statistical Office; Sweden: Statistics Sweden; Switzerland: Office federal des etrangers. Sopemi (1999)

Figure 3
Switzerland, economic growth and immigration 1959–91

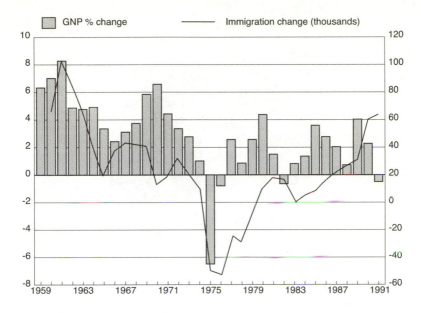

Source: Mauron (1993)

Figure 4
Use of remittances, Bangladesh and Thailand

Bangladesh

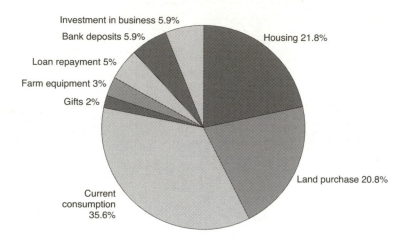

Thailand

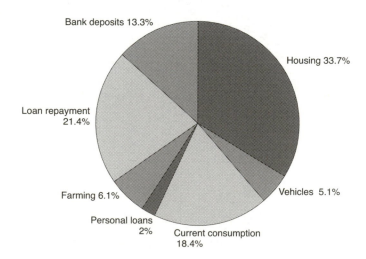

Source: Mahmud (1989)

Further Reading

Asylum Aid (1999), *Still no reason at all: Home Office decisions on Asylum claims*, Asylum Aid, London

Chin, Ko-Lin (1999), *Smuggled Chinese – clandestine immigration to the United States*, Temple University Press, Philadelphia

Dunn, T.J. (1996), *The Militarisation of the US–Mexico Border, 1978–92*, Centre for Mexico–America Studies, University of Texas, Austin

Harris, Nigel (1995), *The New Untouchables, Immigration and the New World Worker*, Tauris / Penguin, London

Morrison, John (2000), *Trafficking and Smuggling of Refugees: The End Game in European Asylum Policy*, UNHCR Policy Research Unit, Geneva, July

OECD (1999), *Trends in International Migration*, SOPEMI–OECD, Paris

Smith, James P. and Barry Edmonston (eds), *The New Americans: Economic, Demographic and Fiscal Effects of Immigration*, National Research Council, National Academy Press, Washington DC

Stalker, Peter (1994), *The Work of Strangers: A Survey of International Labor Migration*, ILO, Geneva

References

Böhning, W.R. (ed.) (1974), *The Effects of the Employment of Foreign Workers*, OECD, Paris

Böhning, W.R. and D. Millat (1972), 'The Social and Occupational Apprenticeship of Mediterranean Migrant Workers in West Germany', in Massimo Livi Bacci (ed.), *The Demographic and Social Patterns of Emigration from Southern European Countries*, University of Florence, Florence

Bonacich, E. and Richard Appelbaum (2000), *Behind the Label: Inequality in the Los Angeles apparel industry*, University of California Press, Berkeley, Los Angeles, London

Eschbach, Karl, Jaqueline Hagan and Nestor Rodriguez (1991), 'Death at the Border', *International Migration Review* 126 (vol. 33), Summer

Hamilton, B. and J. Whalley (1984), 'Efficiency and Distributional Implications of Global Restrictions on Labor Mobility: Calculation and Policy Implications', *Journal of Development Economics* 14

International Organisation for Migration (IOM) (1996), *Trafficking Women in Italy for Sexual Exploitation*, Migration Information Programme, Geneva

Jones, K. and A.D. Smith (1970), *The Economic Impact of Commonwealth Immigration*, Cambridge University Press, Cambridge

Mahmud, W. (1989), 'The Impact of Overseas Labour Migration on the Bangladesh Economy: A Macroeconomic Perspective', in R. Amjad (ed.), *To the Gulf and Back*, ILO, Geneva

Martinez, Vilma S. (1976), 'Illegal Immigration and the Labor Force: An Historic and Legal View', *American Behavioural Scientist* 19, Jan./Feb.

Mauron, T. (1993), *Controlling Immigration with Quotas: Lessons from the Case of Switzerland*, conference paper, *Migration and International Co-operation*, OECD, Paris

Poire, Michael (1976), *Illegal Aliens: An Assessment of the Issues*, National Council on Employment Policy, Washington DC, October

Portes, Alejandro (1974), 'The Return of the Wetback', *Society*, March–April

Reynolds, Clark W. (1979), 'Labor Market Projections for the United States and Mexico, and Their Relevance to Current Migration Controls', *Food Research Institute Studies* 17, Stanford University, Stanford CA

Salt, John and Jeremy Stein (1997), 'Migration as Business: The Case of Trafficking, *International Migration* 34(4), IOM, Geneva

Saxenian, Annalee (1999), *Silicon Valley's New Immigrant Entrepreneurs*, Public Policy Institute of California, Santa Barbara, June

Simon, Rita J. and Susan H. Alexander (1993), *The Ambivalent Welcome: Print Media, Public Opinion and Immigration*, Praeger, Westport CT

Stahl, Charles W. (1989), 'Overview, Economic Perspectives', in Reginald Appleyard (ed.), *The Impact of International Migration on Developing Countries*, Development Centre seminar, OECD, Paris

United Nations Development Programme (1992), *The Human Development Report 1992*, UNDP, New York

US Congress (1990), *US–Mexico Economic Relations: Hearings*, Subcommittee on Trade of the Committee on the Ways and Means, House of Representatives, Serial 101–108, US Government Printing Office, Washington DC

Vantage Point (1999), *Report on the Asylum Decision Process Consultancy* (Ref. IMO/99.215/13), UK Home Office Immigration and Nationality Directorate, July

Widgren, Jonas (1992), *Intergovernmental Consultations on Asylum, Refugee and Migrant Policies in Europe, North America and Australia*, OECD, Paris

Index